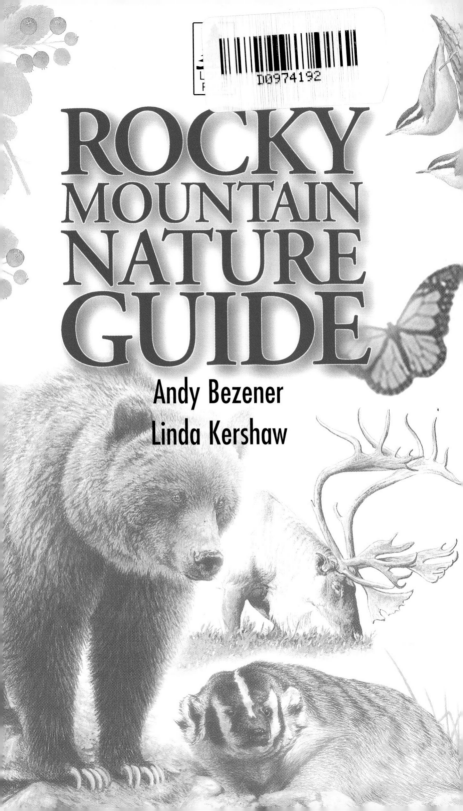

ROCKY
MOUNTAIN
NATURE
GUIDE

Andy Bezener

Linda Kershaw

The Publisher: Lone Pine Publishing

10145 – 81 Ave.	202A, 1110 Seymour St.	1808 B Street NW, Suite 140
Edmonton, AB T6E 1W9	Vancouver, BC V6B 3N3	Auburn, WA 98001
Canada	Canada	USA

Website: www.lonepinepublishing.com

Canadian Cataloguing in Publication Data

Bezener, Andy, 1971–
  Rocky Mountain nature guide

  ISBN 13: 978-1-55105-178-9
  ISBN 10: 1-55105-178-8

  1. Natural history—Rocky Mountains, Canadian (B.C. and Alta.)—Guidebooks.*
2. Rocky Mountains, Canadian (B.C. and Alta.)—Guidebooks.*
I. Kershaw, Linda J., 1951– II. Title.
QH106.2.R6B49 1998   508.711   C98-910982-8

NOTE: This book records many historical uses of plants. Such information is presented to
give the reader a better sense of the rich cultural and natural heritage of this region. This
guide is not meant to be a 'how-to' reference for consuming wild plants. We do not recom-
mend experimentation by readers and we **caution** that many of the plants in the Rocky
Mountains, including some traditional medicines, are **poisonous** and **harmful**.

Editorial Director: Nancy Foulds
Project Editor: Erin McCloskey
Editorial: Erin McCloskey, Lee Craig, Roland Lines
Production Manager: Jody Reekie
Design: Robert Weidemann
Layout & Production: Heather Markham, Jau-Ruey Marvin
Cartography: Volker Bodegom
Scanning, Separations & Film: Elite Lithographers

Cover Illustrations
Grizzly bear, caribou, badger (by Gary Ross); red-breasted nuthatch (by Ted Nordhagen);
monarch butterfly, saskatoon berries (by Ian Sheldon).

Illustrations & Photographs
Mammals & birds by Gary Ross, except Kindrie Grove 46b, 46c, 47b, 49b, 50a, 50c, 51a, 53a,
55a; Horst Krause 34a, 34b; Ted Nordhagen 60a, 61b, 68a, 70a, 71c, 72a, 72c, 75a, 76a, 76b,
78b, 78c, 79a, 80b, 81a, 82a, 82b, 83a, 83c, 84b, 84c, 88a, 88c, 89a, 89b, 90b, 90c, 92a, 93a,
93b, 93c, 94a, 94c, 95a, 95b, 95c; Ewa Pluciennik 64b, 81b.
Reptiles, amphibians, fish, invertebrates & plants by Ian Sheldon, except Gary Ross 96, 98,
99, 100a, 100b, 104a; Linda Dunn 137c, 146a, 148a, 150c; Linda Kershaw 20, 26, 115, 181,
183; Gail Helgason 23.

We acknowledge the financial support of the Government of Canada through the Book
Publishing Industry Development Program (BPIDP) for our publishing activities.

PC:13

CONTENTS

MAMMALS

MOOSE
p. 29

ELK
p. 30

CARIBOU
p. 30

MULE DEER
p. 31

WHITE-TAILED DEER
p. 31

MOUNTAIN GOAT
p. 32

BIGHORN SHEEP
p. 32

GRIZZLY BEAR
p. 33

BLACK BEAR
p. 33

GRAY WOLF
p. 34

COYOTE
p. 34

RED FOX
p. 35

GRAY FOX
p. 35

MOUNTAIN LION
p. 36

LYNX
p. 36

BOBCAT
p. 37

RINGTAIL
p. 37

RACCOON
p. 37

WOLVERINE
p. 38

BADGER
p. 38

NORTHERN RIVER OTTER
p. 38

FISHER
p. 39

MARTEN
p. 39

MINK
p. 39

LONG-TAILED WEASEL
p. 40

SHORT-TAILED WEASEL
p. 40

LEAST WEASEL
p. 40

STRIPED SKUNK
p. 41

WESTERN SPOTTED SKUNK
p. 41

BLACK-TAILED JACKRABBIT
p. 42

WHITE-TAILED JACKRABBIT
p. 42

SHOWSHOE HARE
p. 42

MOUNTAIN COTTONTAIL
p. 43

PIKA
p. 43

PORCUPINE
p. 43

BEAVER
p. 44

MUSKRAT
p. 44

HOARY MARMOT
p. 44

YELLOW-BELLIED MARMOT
p. 45

NORTHERN FLYING
SQUIRREL, p. 45

ABERT'S SQUIRREL
p. 45

RED SQUIRREL
p. 46

ROCK SQUIRREL
p. 46

WYOMING GROUND
SQUIRREL, p. 46

COLUMBIAN GROUND
SQUIRREL, p. 47

UINTA GROUND
SQUIRREL, p. 47

GOLDEN-MANTLED GROUND
SQUIRREL, p. 47

WHITE-TAILED PRAIRIE DOG
p. 48

RED-TAILED CHIPMUNK
p. 48

YELLOW-PINE CHIPMUNK
p. 48

COLORADO CHIPMUNK
p. 49

UINTA CHIPMUNK
p. 49

LEAST CHIPMUNK
p. 49

SOUTHERN RED-BACKED
VOLE, p. 50

5

MAMMALS

HEATHER VOLE
p. 50

LONG-TAILED VOLE
p. 50

MONTANE VOLE
p. 51

MEADOW VOLE
p. 51

WATER VOLE
p. 51

NORTHERN POCKET
GOPHER, p. 52

BUSHY-TAILED WOODRAT
p. 52

NORTHERN BOG
LEMMING, p. 52

WESTERN HARVEST
MOUSE, p. 53

DEER MOUSE
p. 53

HOUSE MOUSE
p. 53

NORWAY RAT
p. 54

ORD'S KANGAROO RAT
p. 54

WESTERN JUMPING MOUSE
p. 54

WATER SHREW
p. 55

DUSKY SHREW
p. 55

PYGMY SHREW
p. 55

WESTERN LONG-EARED MYOTIS
p. 56

LITTLE BROWN MYOTIS
p. 56

HOARY BAT
p. 56

SILVER-HAIRED BAT
p. 57

BIG BROWN BAT
p. 57

TOWNSEND'S BIG-EARED
BAT, p. 57

BIRDS

COMMON LOON
p. 59

EARED GREBE
p. 60

WESTERN GREBE
p. 60

GREAT BLUE HERON
p. 60

SANDHILL CRANE
p. 61

SORA
p. 61

AMERICAN COOT
p. 61

TRUMPETER SWAN
p. 62

CANADA GOOSE
p. 62

MALLARD
p. 62

NORTHERN PINTAIL
p. 63

BLUE-WINGED TEAL
p. 63

HARLEQUIN DUCK
p. 64

BARROW'S GOLDENEYE
p. 64

RUDDY DUCK
p. 65

HOODED MERGANSER
p. 65

COMMON MERGANSER
p. 65

TURKEY VULTURE
p. 66

BALD EAGLE
p. 66

GOLDEN EAGLE
p. 66

OSPREY
p. 67

NORTHERN GOSHAWK
p. 67

RED-TAILED HAWK
p. 67

AMERICAN KESTREL
p. 68

PEREGRINE FALCON
p. 68

GREAT HORNED OWL
p. 68

GREAT GRAY OWL
p. 69

BLUE GROUSE
p. 69

WHITE-TAILED PTARMIGAN
p. 69

KILLDEER
p. 70

SPOTTED SANDPIPER
p. 70

CALIFORNIA GULL
p. 70

FORSTER'S TERN
p. 71

ROCK DOVE
p. 71

MOURNING DOVE
p. 71

RED-NAPED SAPSUCKER
p. 72

DOWNY WOODPECKER
p. 72

THREE-TOED WOODPECKER
p. 72

NORTHERN FLICKER
p. 73

PILEATED WOODPECKER
p. 73

COMMON NIGHTHAWK
p. 74

BELTED KINGFISHER
p. 74

CALLIOPE HUMMINGBIRD
p. 75

BROAD-TAILED HUMMINGBIRD, p. 75

RUFOUS HUMMINGBIRD
p. 75

OLIVE-SIDED FLYCATCHER
p. 76

EASTERN KINGBIRD
p. 76

WHITE-THROATED SWIFT
p. 77

VIOLET-GREEN SWALLOW
p. 77

BARN SWALLOW
p. 77

GRAY JAY
p. 78

STELLER'S JAY
p. 78

WESTERN SCRUB-JAY
p. 78

CLARK'S NUTCRACKER
p. 79

BLACK-BILLED MAGPIE
p. 79

COMMON RAVEN
p. 79

BLACK-CAPPED CHICKADEE, p. 80

MOUNTAIN CHICKADEE
p. 80

RED-BREASTED NUTHATCH
p. 81

WHITE-BREASTED
NUTHATCH, p. 81

BROWN CREEPER
p. 81

ROCK WREN
p. 82

HOUSE WREN
p. 82

RUBY-CROWNED KINGLET
p. 83

GOLDEN-CROWNED
KINGLET, p. 83

BLUE-GRAY GNATCATCHER
p. 83

MOUNTAIN BLUEBIRD
p. 84

TOWNSEND'S SOLITAIRE
p. 84

AMERICAN ROBIN
p. 84

VARIED THRUSH
p. 85

PLUMBEOUS VIREO
p. 85

WESTERN TANAGER
p. 85

YELLOW-RUMPED WARBLER
p. 86

YELLOW WARBLER
p. 86

TOWNSEND'S WARBLER
p. 86

AMERICAN REDSTART
p. 87

COMMON YELLOWTHROAT
p. 87

WILSON'S WARBLER
p. 87

HORNED LARK
p. 88

EUROPEAN STARLING
p. 88

LOGGERHEAD SHRIKE
p. 88

GRAY CATBIRD
p. 89

CEDAR WAXWING
p. 89

AMERICAN DIPPER
p. 89

SPOTTED TOWHEE
p. 90

CHIPPING SPARROW
p. 90

VESPER SPARROW
p. 90

SONG SPARROW
p. 91

WHITE-CROWNED
SPARROW, p. 91

DARK-EYED JUNCO
p. 91

YELLOW-HEADED BLACKBIRD
p. 92

RED-WINGED BLACKBIRD
p. 92

WESTERN MEADOWLARK
p. 92

BROWN-HEADED COWBIRD
p. 93

BULLOCK'S ORIOLE
p. 93

RED CROSSBILL
p. 93

GRAY-CROWNED
ROSY-FINCH, p. 94

HOUSE FINCH
p. 94

AMERICAN GOLDFINCH
p. 94

EVENING GROSBEAK
p. 95

LAZULI BUNTING
p. 95

HOUSE SPARROW
p. 95

TIGER SALAMANDER
p. 96

WESTERN LONG-TOED
SALAMANDER, p. 97

PACIFIC GIANT SALAMANDER
p. 97

VAN DYKE'S SALAMANDER
p. 97

TAILED FROG
p. 98

GREAT BASIN SPADEFOOT
p. 98

NORTHERN LEOPARD FROG
p. 98

SPOTTED FROG
p. 99

WOOD FROG
p. 99

WESTERN TOAD
p. 99

PACIFIC TREEFROG
p. 100

BOREAL CHORUS FROG
p. 100

WESTERN PAINTED TURTLE
p. 100

EASTERN SHORT-HORNED LIZARD
p. 101

SAGEBRUSH LIZARD
p. 101

NORTHERN ALLIGATOR LIZARD
p. 101

WESTERN SKINK
p. 102

RUBBER BOA
p. 102

YELLOW-BELLIED RACER
p. 102

WESTERN SMOOTH GREEN
SNAKE, p. 103

GREAT BASIN GOPHER SNAKE
p. 103

WESTERN TERRESTIAL GARTER SNAKE
p. 103

COMMON GARTER SNAKE
p. 104

WESTERN RATTLESNAKE
p. 104

CHINOOK SALMON
p. 105

RAINBOW TROUT
p. 106

CUTTHROAT TROUT
p. 106

GOLDEN TROUT
p. 106

LAKE TROUT
p. 107

BULL TROUT
p. 107

BROOK TROUT
p. 107

BROWN TROUT
p. 108

MOUNTAIN WHITEFISH
p. 108

FISH

ARCTIC GRAYLING
p. 108

LAKE CHUB
p. 109

LONGNOSE DACE
p. 109

LONGNOSE SUCKER
p. 109

ANT
p. 110

MOSQUITO
p. 110

CADDISFLY
p. 110

INVERTEBRATES

DRAGONFLY
p. 111

PREDACEOUS DIVING BEETLE
p. 111

WOOD TICK
p. 111

MONARCH BUTTERFLY
p. 112

WEIDEMEYER'S ADMIRAL
p. 112

MOURNING CLOAK
p. 112

ANISE SWALLOWTAIL
p. 113

SPRING AZURE
p. 113

CLOUDED SULPHUR
p. 113

BASALM POPLAR
p. 116

TREMBLING ASPEN
p. 116

WHITE BIRCH
p. 117

PONDEROSA PINE
p. 117

TREES

LIMBER PINE
p. 118

LODGEPOLE PINE
p. 118

WESTERN LARCH
p. 119

DOUGLAS-FIR
p. 119

SUBALPINE FIR
p. 120

TREES

| Engelmann Spruce p. 120 | Western Hemlock p. 121 | Western Red Cedar p. 121 | Rocky Mountain Juniper, p. 123 | Common Juniper p. 123 |

SHRUBS

| Western Yew p. 123 | Scouler's Willow p. 124 | Rocky Mountain Maple p. 124 | Green Alder p. 124 |

| Squaw Currant p. 125 | Bristly Black Currant p. 125 | Creeping Oregon-grape p. 125 | Common Snowberry p. 126 |

| Utah Honeysuckle p. 126 | Bracted Honeysuckle p. 126 | Black Elderberry p. 127 | Choke Cherry p. 127 |

| Saskatoon p. 127 | Birch-leaved Spirea p. 128 | Thimbleberry p. 128 | Prickly Rose p. 128 |

| Western Mountain-ash p. 129 | Shrubby Cinquefoil p. 129 | Red-osier Dogwood p. 129 | Silverberry p. 130 |

SHRUBS

CANADA BUFFALOBERRY
p. 130

FALSEBOX
p. 130

BIG SAGEBRUSH
p. 131

COMMON RABBITBUSH
p. 131

PINK MOUNTAIN-HEATHER
p. 131

COMMON BEARBERRY
p. 132

GROUSEBERRY
p. 132

BLACK HUCKLEBERRY
p. 132

FALSE AZALEA
p. 133

PRINCE'S-PINE
p. 133

BEARGRASS
p. 136

MOUNTAIN DEATH-CAMAS
p. 136

HERBS

NODDING ONION
p. 136

THREE-SPOTTED MARIPOSA-LILY
p. 137

WESTERN TRILLIUM
p. 137

WESTERN WOOD LILY
p. 137

YELLOW GLACIER-LILY
p. 138

CORN-LILY
p. 138

STAR-FLOWERED FALSE
SOLOMON'S-SEAL, p. 138

ROUGH-FRUITED FAIRYBELLS
p. 139

CLASPING-LEAVED TWISTED-STALK
p. 139

GREEN FALSE-HELLEBORE
p. 139

WESTERN RATTLESNAKE-PLANTAIN
p. 140

FIREWEED
p. 140

SITKA VALERIAN
p. 140

COW-PARSNIP
p. 141

WHITE ANGELICA
p. 141

SULPHUR BUCKWHEAT
p. 141

NORTHERN BEDSTRAW
p. 142

MOSS CAMPION
p. 142

FIELD CHICKWEED
p. 142

CUT-LEAVED FOAMFLOWER
p. 143

SPOTTED SAXIFRAGE
p. 143

FRINGED GRASS-OF-
PARNASSUS, p. 143

WESTERN SPRINGBEAUTY
p. 144

BUNCHBERRY
p. 144

WHITE MOUNTAIN-AVENS
p. 144

WILD STRAWBERRY
p. 145

DIVERSE-LEAVED
CINQUEFOIL, p. 145

OLD MAN'S WHISKERS
p. 145

ROCKY MOUNTAIN
COW-LILY, p. 146

CUT-LEAVED ANEMONE
p. 146

YELLOW COLUMBINE
p. 146

WESTERN MEADOWRUE
p. 147

BANEBERRY
p. 147

BLUE VIRGIN'S BOWER
p. 147

SILKY LUPINE
p. 148

SHOWY LOCOWEED
p. 148

YELLOW SWEET-VETCH
p. 148

NORTHERN SWEET-VETCH
p. 149

ALPINE MILK-VETCH
p. 149

WILD VETCH
p. 149

EARLY BLUE VIOLET
p. 150

ROUND-LEAVED YELLOW
VIOLET, p. 150

HERBS

WILD BERGAMOT
p. 150

SPREADING DOGBANE
p. 151

COMMON HAREBELL
p. 151

SILKY SCORPIONWEED
p. 151

LANCE-LEAVED STONECROP
p. 152

SLENDER BLUE PENSTEMON
p. 152

YELLOW MONKEY-FLOWER
p. 152

SICKLETOP LOUSEWORT
p. 153

BRACTED LOUSEWORT
p. 153

SCARLET PAINTBRUSH
p. 153

LEMONWEED
p. 154

WESTERN BLUE FLAX
p. 154

STICKY PURPLE GERANIUM
p. 154

PINK WINTERGREEN
p. 155

GREENISH-FLOWERED
WINTERGREEN, p. 155

TWINFLOWER
p. 155

SUBALPINE FLEABANE
p. 156

SHOWY ASTER
p. 156

CANADA GOLDENROD
p. 156

ARROW-LEAVED
GROUNDSEL, p. 157

CURLY-CUP GUMWEED
p. 157

HEART-LEAVED ARNICA
p. 157

ARROW-LEAVED
BASALMROOT, p. 158

BROWN-EYED SUSAN
p. 158

PEARLY EVERLASTING
p. 158

YARROW
p. 159

RACEMOSE PUSSYTOES
p. 159

SLENDER HAWKWEED
p. 159

ORANGE AGOSERIS
p. 160

MEADOW BUTTERCUP
p. 160

BUTTER-AND-EGGS
p. 160

GREAT MULLEIN
p. 160

YELLOW SWEET-CLOVER
p. 160

ALFALFA
p. 161

RED CLOVER
p. 161

ALSIKE CLOVER
p. 161

WHITE CLOVER
p. 161

TEASEL
p. 161

OXEYE DAISY
p. 161

PINEAPPLE WEED
p. 161

COMMON TANSY
p. 161

ANNUAL HAWKSBEARD
p. 161

YELLOW SALISFY
p. 161

PERENNIAL SOW-THISTLE
p. 161

COMMON DANDELION
p. 161

CHICORY
p. 161

SPOTTED KNAPWEED
p. 161

CANADA THISTLE
p. 161

BULL THISTLE
p. 161

Tens of millions of people visit the Rocky Mountains each year to feast on scenic vistas and re-energize their souls. Those who have lived among or traveled through North America's magnificent Rockies will never forget the incredible beauty and rich diversity of life found here. Renowned for massive glaciers, high, snow-capped peaks, turquoise-blue lakes, rushing, crystal-clear streams, sparkling waterfalls, and unbroken expanses of deep green forests, the Rockies are one of the few places in North America that still provide us with a vision of wildness. But beyond the spectacular landscape features, the Rockies hold a secret magic within the plant and animal communities found here and nowhere else on earth. When you visit the Rocky Mountains, it will become apparent to you how the plants and animals are integral components of this ecosystem.

Many of us are thrilled by the sight of brilliant summer wildflowers and lush green trees, vivid butterflies, fish, reptiles and amphibians, colorful birds, and curious mammals. By learning to identify the species and their various roles in this ecosystem, our Rocky Mountain experience becomes much more rewarding. This guide is for people who have found beauty and wonder in the Rocky Mountains and have longed to understand more about its wild inhabitants. We hope this guide will enhance your encounters with the plants and animals of these mountains, inspire you to understand their importance, and allow you to discover first-hand the true joy and wonder of the Rockies.

ROCKY MOUNTAIN GEOLOGY

The Rocky Mountains are a dominant landscape feature of North America, forming the continent's backbone— the Continental Divide. This height of land separates waters flowing to the Pacific Ocean from waters flowing to either the Arctic Ocean or the Gulf of Mexico. Some of North America's largest rivers begin as glaciers or small streams in the Rocky Mountains. This chain of mountains is approximately 250–345 mi (400–550 km) wide and stretches over 3000 mi (4800 km) in length— from the Sacramento Mountains of New Mexico to the Brooks Range in Alaska and the Selwyn and Mackenzie mountains in the Yukon and Northwest Territories. These mountains transcend arbitrary political boundaries as they span across two countries and seven states, two provinces, and two territories.

This guide focuses on the Rockies (and the Columbia Mountains) from the Liard River in northern British Columbia to the Sangre de Cristo Mountain Range north of Santa Fe, New Mexico. This area is commonly divided into three segments: the Canadian Rockies, the Northern U.S. Rockies, and the Southern U.S. Rockies; where the species are found will be identified more specifically in this book.

The geological history of the Rockies is a fascinating and complex story that scientists are still piecing together. This history is estimated to have spanned no less than 1.5 billion years. Geological study indicates that different parts of the Rockies were formed at different times and in different ways. Vertical thrusting and faulting of sedimentary rocks that were once the bed of an ancient sea formed some of the Rocky Mountain ranges. Some ranges are made of metamorphic rocks that formed under-ground under tremendous heat and pressure before becoming exposed to the surface, while other ranges are composed of igneous rocks created by volcanic processes.

More recently, continental glaciers sculpted many of these mountain ranges into the deep, U-shaped valleys, steep slopes, and high peaks we see today. The remnants of these glaciers still cover many of the mountain crests in the Canadian and Northern U.S. Rockies. The highest mountain peaks in the Rocky Mountains are found in the southern U.S. segment, with 54 summits reaching over 14,000 ft (4270 m) above sea level. As you can imagine, each of the three segments of the Rockies displays unique scenic and biological characteristics based on each segment's unique geological history.

BIOLOGICAL (LIFE) ZONES

T he Rocky Mountains contain different growing environments, known as 'biological zones' or 'life zones.' Biological zones are the product of unique combinations of geology, climate, elevation, latitude, slope direction (aspect), and slope angle. The following section lists these zones and the plants and animals found within them.

Alpine (Tundra) Zone

This zone comprises the bare rocks, glaciers, tundra, and alpine meadows above treeline. This cold, windswept environment may have snow-free areas early in spring and even through most of winter, but the alpine can lay blanketed with drifts for most or all of summer. The temperature is just high enough for enough days to permit vegetative growth. At treeline, the ground is thawed long enough for the trees to gain their yearly supply of soil moisture and minerals, and summer growth barely replaces needles and twigs killed in winter. Fewer species of plants and animals survive in the alpine than in other ecoregions. The high mountain peaks of the Rocky Mountains are some of the highest in the world and they call out to climbers who

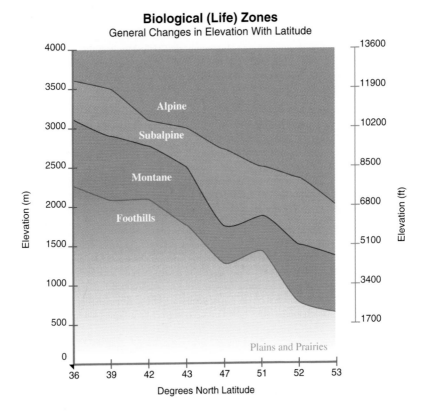

Biological (Life) Zones
General Changes in Elevation With Latitude

dare to attempt to conquer them. The highest peak in the Rocky Mountains is Mount Elbert in Colorado at 14,433 ft (4399 m) above sea level with an ascent of 2400 ft (731.5 m) from the base to the peak. Mount Robson in B.C. is at 12,972 ft (3954 m) above sea level, but it has a more significant ascent (9741 ft [2969 m] from base to peak). With its summit being only 2½ mi (4 km) from its base at Kinney Lake, Mount Robson provides a neck-breaking perspective.

Lush alpine meadows, dry, rocky slopes and glacier-fed cirque lakes support a diversity of plants and animals:

- Sedges (*Carex* spp.), arrow-leaved groundsel, Sitka valerian, scarlet paintbrush, anemones, moss campion, white mountain-avens, alpine milk-vetch, northern sweet-vetch, diverse-leaved cinquefoil, and spotted saxifrage
- golden trout, golden eagle, white-tailed ptarmigan, calliope hummingbird, horned lark, gray-crowned rosy-finch, hoary marmot, wolverine, and mountain goat.

Subalpine Zone

This zone exists upward from the upper edge of the montane to treeline and consists of dense clumps of evergreens and wildflower meadows. Mid-elevation slopes have heavy forests with cool, damp, mossy forest floors and receive the heaviest snow accumulation. Farther upslope the trees become shorter or shrub-like, often on the eastern, leeward side of rocks and ridges where the trees are more sheltered under the snow and can therefore escape winds and winter storms. These trees are often called 'kruppelholz' or 'krummholz.' The subalpine is what most people envision when they think of the Rocky Mountains. Stunning waterfalls, rocky cliffs dotted with mountain goats, and golden eagles soaring against an impressive backdrop of towering mountain peaks are a few of the spectacular images this ecoregion offers. Travelers often visit the subalpine's ski resorts and secluded cabins to add adventure and romance to their mountain vacation.

Dense and almost continuous forests of subalpine fir and Engelmann spruce, with mossy forest floors, support a range of flora and fauna including:

- yellow columbine, pink wintergreen, glacier-lily, cow-parsnip, subalpine fleabane, twinflower, grouseberry, black elderberry, Canada buffaloberry, limber pine, and whitebark pine (*Pinus albicaulis*)
- western long-toed salamander, spotted frog, harlequin duck, blue grouse, broad-tailed hummingbird, American dipper, Clark's nutcracker, Townsend's solitaire, yellow-pine chipmunk, water vole, grizzly bear, and bighorn sheep.

Montane Zone

This zone consists of the lower slopes and valleys above the foothills. The western slopes are wetter, heavier, and shrubbier compared to the drier eastern slopes. The montane also holds the greatest variety of wildflowers, trees, and shrubs. In Canada montane valley floors exist along major eastern-slope rivers such as the Bow, the North Saskatchewan, and the Athabasca. These valleys are critical winter habitat for elk, deer, and bighorn sheep, and therefore also for their predators such as the wolf and the coyote. This habitat is essential but small (only 2–10 percent of the Canadian Rockies). Unfortunately, this same 2–10 percent of the Rockies is favored by humans. It is in the montane that the heaviest effects of human encroachment occur. Such effects include roads and freeways, railways, resorts, campgrounds, towns such as Banff and Jasper, convention centers, golf courses, and cross-country ski trails. For these reasons, many conflicts between humans and wildlife have occurred and predator and prey populations have been separated in some areas. In the U.S. the montane zone meadows are heavily used for agriculture and grazing or have been altered by fire suppression, while the wetlands are affected by irrigation and diversion. The montane is a threatened ecoregion in need of protection and restoration.

Open stands of lodgepole pine, ponderosa pine, Douglas-fir, limber pine, white spruce, and/or trembling aspen with sunny understories of grasses, wildflowers, and low shrubs support:
- Junegrass (*Kolelaria macrantha*), pearly everlasting, common harebell, heart-leaved arnica, falsebox, common bearberry, and common juniper
- elk, bison, deer, cougar, wolf, and great gray owl.

Foothills Zone

This zone is the transition from the plains and prairies to the mountains. The first low-elevation slopes before the treed montane slopes are considered the foothills. In northern Canada the transition is less distinct: the foothills blend into the boreal forest in the east and the Columbian forest in the west. In the U.S. the foothills are generally low-elevation scrublands that blend into the prairies. The cooler, moister, north-facing slopes and valleys are where shrubs first grow, but with increasing elevation they spread to south-facing slopes. Trees then begin to appear on the northern slopes and valleys and eventually they become the montane forests. Grasses provide scattered ground cover in these dry communities.

Foothill communities vary dramatically from northern Canada to the southern U.S. For the Canadian Rockies, species include:
- lodgepole pine, white spruce, trembling aspen, Canada buffaloberry, prickly rose, and common bearberry
- mourning cloak, brook trout, western toad, western terrestrial, garter snake, trumpeter swan, sandhill crane, pileated woodpecker, beaver, elk, woodland caribou, and black bear.

For the Northern U.S. Rockies, species include:
- juniper, sagebrush, chokecherry, saskatoon, arrow-leaved balsamroot, and penstemons
- tiger salamander, bullsnake, red-tailed hawk, black-billed magpie, lazuli bunting, vesper sparrow, white-tailed jackrabbit, northern pocket gopher, mule deer, and bobcat.

Species in the southern U.S. Rockies include:
- blue gramma (*Bouteloua gracilis*), Indian ricegrass (*Oryzopsis hymenoides*), prickly-pear cactus (*Opuntia* ssp.), gumweeds (*Grindelia* spp.), golden-aster (*Heterotheca villosa*), and fleabanes (*Erigeron* spp.).
- Great Basin spadefoot, western smooth green snake, American kestrel, western scrub jay, mountain bluebird, spotted towhee, Ord's kangaroo rat, mountain cottontail, and long-tailed weasel.

Plains and Prairies

This zone is the only one that is technically not part of the Rocky Mountains. The plains and prairies lie in the rainshadow east of the Rockies and blend into the foothills but do not form a definite zone within the mountains. Scattered tracts of grassland can be found almost anywhere in the Rockies south of the Athabasca Valley in Jasper National Park.

These grasslands provide homes for:
- fescues (*Festuca* spp.), wheatgrasses (*Agropyron* spp.), blue grama (*Bouteloua gracilis*), Junegrass (*Koeleria macrantha*), needle-and-thread grass (*Stipa comata*), sagebrush (*Artemesia* spp.), big sagebrush, and common rabbitbrush
- grasshoppers, brown trout, northern leopard frog, western rattlesnake, loggerhead shrike, brown-headed cowbird, western meadowlark, prairie dog, western harvest mouse, and badger.

Many species such as the grizzly bear, elk, and mountain lion, were once widespread across the plains until their populations were exterminated by settlers.

Human-altered Landscapes

Many of the most common plants and animals found along roads, in fields, and around townsites did not live here less than 200 years ago. These highly successful exotics were introduced to North America from Europe and Asia by humans:
- spotted knapweed, chicory, oxeye daisy, pineapple weed, perennial sow-thistle, common tansy, common dandelion, alfalfa, meadow buttercup, great mullein, and sweet-clover
- seven-spot ladybird beetles, house sparrows, European starlings, house mice, Norway rats, and big brown bats.

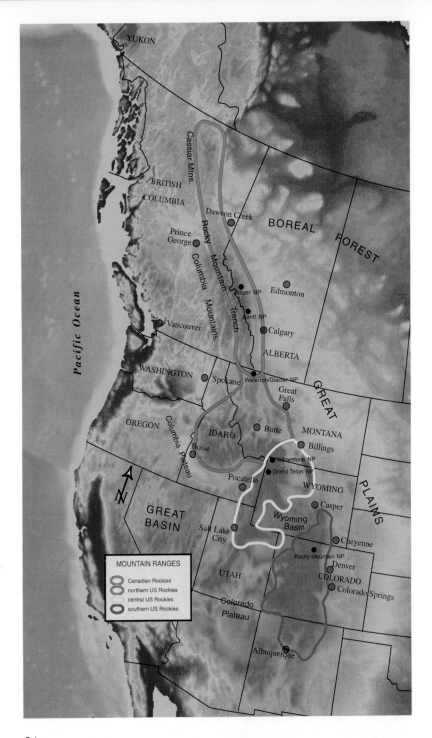

HOW TO USE THIS BOOK

Quick identification measurements are listed at the beginning of each species account. Dimensions given for fauna are for length meaning 'total length including tail,' and for larger mammals the height is also given, which is measured from ground to shoulder level. Wingspans are provided for bats and butterflies. Dimensions given for flora are for total height as well as for additional features diagnostic to that plant.

The back pages briefly describe seasons and climate, parks and protected areas, people in the Rockies, and nature ethics. The Parks & Protected Areas section includes maps of the states and provinces whose borders include the Rockies and descriptions of important and accessible national, state and provincial parks, national monuments, wilderness areas, and recreation areas. Use the indexed color tabs to find groups of similar plants and animals for quick and easy species identification. The glossary near the back of the book defines technical terms used in the species accounts.

ENJOYING ROCKY MOUNTAIN NATURE

Many millions of people from around the world flock to the Rockies each year to experience scenic vistas, fresh air, and wilderness. It is easy to imagine the effect such a large number of admirers could have on plants, animals, and the landscape. Practicing minimum-impact techniques such as those listed below will help keep the Rockies clean, beautiful, and wild for people, plants, and animals:

1. Avoid approaching, harassing, or feeding wildlife. Wildlife that learn to associate people with food can become aggressive and dangerous once they have stopped foraging for natural foods. Pets that chase or kill wildlife are best left at home.

2. Stay on designated trails and camping sites. These sites have been hardened to bear the impact of repeated human use. There is minimal impact on vegetation and fewer animal conflicts when people stay on the trails.

3. Bring your eyes to the flower, not the flower to your eyes. Picking flowers and removing them can damage or kill the plant and prevent others from enjoying its beauty. Similar respect should be shown toward fossils, artifacts, antlers, and other sources of natural history.

4. Leave wild animals in their natural habitat. Removing wildlife from wild places almost always results in more harm than good.

5. Keep your food secure from animals, keep your cooking materials clean and dispose of your garbage in designated animal-proof containers. Resist littering! Backcountry campers should pack out all of their garbage rather than burying it or leaving it in the backcountry.

6. Respect the rights of landowners and other wildlife viewers. Ask permission to access private lands and respect the rules of public lands.

ANIMALS

Animals are mammals, birds, reptiles, fish, and invertebrates all of which belong to the Kingdom Animalia. They obtain energy by ingesting food that they hunt or gather. They are endothermic: the body temperature is internally regulated and will stay nearly constant despite the surrounding environmental temperature unless that temperature is extreme and persistent. They reproduce sexually and they have a limited growth that is reached at sexual maturity. Animals have diverse and complicated behaviors displayed in courtship, defense, parenting, playing, fighting, eating, hunting, in their social hierarchy, and in how they deal with stresses in their environments such as weather, change of season, or availability of food and water.

GUIDE TO THE MAMMAL GROUPS

HOOFED MAMMALS
pp. 29–32

BEARS
p. 33

DOGS
pp. 34–35

CATS
pp. 36–37

RACCOON & KIN
p. 37

WEASELS
pp. 38–41

RABBITS, HARES & KIN
pp. 42–43

PORCUPINE
p. 43

BEAVER & MUSKRAT
p. 44

SQUIRRELS
pp. 44–49

VOLES
pp. 50–51

RATS, MICE & KIN
pp. 52–54

SHREWS
p. 55

BATS
pp. 56–57

MAMMALS

Mammals are the group to which human beings belong. The general characteristics of a mammal include being endothermic, bearing live young (with the exception of the platypus), nursing their young, and having hair or fur on their bodies. In general, all mammals larger than rodents are sexually dimorphic, meaning that the male and the female are different in appearance by size or other diagnostics such as antlers. Males are usually larger than females. Different groups of mammals are either herbivores, carnivores, omnivores, or insectivores. People often associate large mammals with wilderness, making them prominent symbols in native legend and stirring emotional connections with people in modern times.

Moose

Alces alces

LENGTH: 6½–9 ft (2–2.7 m)
HEIGHT: 5½–6 ft (1.7–1.8 m)

The largest deer in the world, moose have been known to dive to depths of over 13 ft (4 m) to find aquatic plants rich in salts and minerals...and to escape those nasty biting insects! Moose browse on trees and shrubs, and graze on grasses and forbs. Long legs and high steps make the moose well adapted for walking through bogs and deep snow without expending excess energy. **Where found:** in and around lakes, bogs, and riparian valleys; also in young deciduous, mixed, and coniferous forests; from B.C. and Alberta to northern Colorado.

Elk

Cervus elaphus
LENGTH: 6–9 ft (1.8–2.7 m)
HEIGHT: 4–5 ft (1.2–1.5 m)

Sounding like haunting cries from ancient forest spirits, the high-pitched bugle calls of rutting male elk are a hallmark of autumn in the Rocky Mountains. Elk tend to be shy forest dwellers, moving to open meadows at dusk to feed until dawn. A male's large, spreading antlers may span 5 ft (1.5 m) and weigh up to 30 lb (14 kg). During fall rut and in spring when hinds (females) are with calves, elk can be very dangerous and should be avoided. **Where found:** mixed forests, coniferous forests, mountain meadows, and lake shorelines up to timberline; throughout the Rockies. **Also known as:** wapiti.

Woodland Caribou

Rangifer tarandus
LENGTH: 4½–7½ ft (1.4–2.3 m)
HEIGHT: 3½–4 ft (1.1–1.2 m)

Woodland caribou are the only members of the Deer Family in which both sexes grow antlers: the female's are slender and the male's are large and C-shaped. Large, crescent-shaped hooves, a long throat mane and well-furred ears and muzzle make caribou superbly adapted for surviving harsh winters. Caribou migrate to different elevations between seasons. In winter, tree lichens form the bulk of their diet. **Where found:** old-growth coniferous forests of the subalpine and on alpine tundra; small populations in the Canadian Rockies and northern Idaho.

Mule Deer
Odocoileus hemionus

LENGTH: 4–6½ ft (1.2–2 m)
HEIGHT: 3–3½ ft (91–107 cm)

More gregarious than the white-tailed deer, mule deer form large bands particularly in winter. They prefer hilly terrain where they use bounding hops like those of jackrabbits to escape predators. These deer are named for their very large, mule-like ears. Large ears and a black-tipped tail are the best field marks for this ungulate. **Where found:** lower grasslands, montane valleys, riparian areas, and mixed or coniferous forests up to sub-alpine; throughout the Rockies. **Also known as:** black-tailed deer.

White-tailed Deer
Odocoileus virginianus

LENGTH: 5½–7 ft (1.7–2.1 m)
HEIGHT: 3–3½ ft (91–107 cm)

A wagging white tail disappearing into the forest is a common view of this abundant and adaptable deer. When a mother deer is feeding, it will leave its scentless, spotted fawn behind among tall grasses or shrubs to hide it from potential preda-tors. A dense network of blood vessels coated by hair, called velvet, covers the developing antlers of males in spring and summer. **Where found:** pri-marily in forests and along forest edges at lower eleva-tions; throughout most of the Rockies, except in some areas of Utah, Colorado, and New Mexico. **Also known as:** Virginia deer.

Mountain Goat

Oreamnos americanus

LENGTH: 4–6½ ft (1.2–2 m)
HEIGHT: 3–3½ ft (91–107 cm)

Watching mountain goats climbing or descending the steep rocky slopes of their high alpine home can leave observers breathless. Usually found as solitary individuals or in small groups, they can often be seen at natural, lower elevation mineral licks in the early morning or late evening. Within hours of being born, playful mountain goat kids are able to run, jump, and climb. **Where found:** high-elevation meadows, cliffs, and talus slopes, usually at or above treeline; from B.C. and Alberta to Wyoming.

Bighorn Sheep

Ovis canadensis

LENGTH: 5–6 ft (1.5–1.8 m)
HEIGHT: 3–4 ft (91–122 cm)

Mountain meadows provide feeding grounds, and rocky outcroppings provide protection from predators for bighorn sheep. Males are known for their spectacular head-butting clashes during fall rut. The horns of sheep are composed of a bony core and an outer shell of keratin—the same material that forms our hair and fingernails. Both sexes have brown horns, but males' are thick and curved forward. **Where found:** rugged mountain slopes, cliffs, and alpine meadows; some populations in rolling foothills; throughout the Rockies. **Also known as:** mountain sheep, Rocky Mountain bighorn sheep.

Grizzly Bear
Ursus arctos
LENGTH: 6–8 ft (1.8–2.6 m)
HEIGHT: 3–4 ft (91–122 cm)

To many people, the grizzly bear is the ultimate symbol of wildness. Plants and carrion make up most of its omnivorous diet. Grizzlies migrate from low elevation valleys to high alpine meadows between seasons, sleeping through the winter months in high elevation dens they dig each fall. The coat varies from pale yellow to dark brown. Grizzlies have a prominent shoulder hump and a dished face, and their long front claws are always visible, so they can easily be distinguished from black bears (below). A suprised mother grizzly with cubs can be very dangerous: hikers are advised to practice bear avoidance techniques to protect both people and bears. **Where found:** forests and riparian areas in valley bottoms to high alpine tundra and avalanche slopes in isolated wilderness; from Yellowstone National Park north. **Also known as:** brown bear.

Black Bear
Ursus americanus
LENGTH: 4½–6 ft (1.4–1.8 m)
HEIGHT: 3–3½ ft (91–107 cm)

The black bear is the most common bear of the Rockies. Dormant bears overwintering in their dens are able to recycle their own waste products into usable proteins until they emerge from their sleep in spring. They are excellent climbers whose molar teeth are remarkably similar to those of humans. Their pelage is most commonly black but varies to cinnamon-brown, white, or bluish-white, always with a white 'V' on the chest. Black bears have a lighter colored muzzle and an evenly sloping facial profile. **Where found:** forests, marshes, riparian areas, alpine meadows, and avalanche slopes; throughout the Rockies.

Gray Wolf
Canis lupus

LENGTH: 60–78 in (1.5–2 m)
HEIGHT: 26–38 in (66–97 cm)

The hauntingly beautiful howl of the wolf is a unique and vital wilderness sound. This species is often wide-ranging—1 wolf identified in the mountains of Idaho turned up in Alberta's Banff National Park. Wolf packs have a strong social hierarchy with a dominant (alpha) male and female, which are often the only breeding pair in the pack. Wolves have gray, white, or occasionally black pelage. They have a thicker, wider muzzle than coyotes (below) and hold their tails high when running. **Where found:** in a variety of habitats in remote wilderness areas; from Yellowstone National Park north. **Also known as:** timber wolf.

Coyote
Canis latrans

LENGTH: 40–52 in (1–1.3 m)
HEIGHT: 23–26 in (58–66 cm)

Occasionally forming loose packs and joining in spirited yipping choruses, coyotes are intelligent and versatile hunter-scavengers. Coyotes are best described as opportunistic omnivores. They have been observed fishing or even engaging the help of a hunting badger to catch ground squirrels. The fur on the back and tail is gray to reddish-brown, with lighter ears, forelegs, feet, and muzzle. The tail drags behind the coyote's legs when it is running. **Where found:** mixed and coniferous forests, meadows, and agricultural lands; throughout the Rockies. **Also known as:** brush wolf, prairie wolf.

Red Fox
Vulpes vulpes

LENGTH: 36–42 in (91–107 cm)
HEIGHT: 15 in (38 cm)

Red foxes are talented and entertaining mousers. Patient observers are treated to the high-pouncing antics of a fox hunting for small rodents on an isolated alpine meadow or forest edge. Its coat has three color phases: red phase (reddish-yellow with black feet); black phase (black, often with white-tipped hairs); and cross phase (brown to reddish-yellow with a blackish cross down the back and shoulders). All phases have a thick, white-tipped tail. **Where found:** in many different habitats, including forests, meadows, alpine tundra, riparian areas, and forest edges; throughout the Rockies.

Gray Fox
Urocyon cinereoargenteus

LENGTH: 30–43 in (76–110 cm)
HEIGHT: 14–15 in (36–38 cm)

Preferring rocky, shrub-covered terrain, and avoiding populated areas, the mainly nocturnal gray fox is seldom seen by human observers. Most remarkable is its ability to climb trees to escape danger, pursue birds, or find egg-filled nests. Gray foxes may even use a high tree-hollow for denning. Like other foxes, it is omnivorous. The gray fox's fur is shorter and denser than that of the red fox (above). **Where found:** open forests, shrublands, and rocky areas; Utah, Colorado, and New Mexico.

Mountain Lion
Felis concolor

LENGTH: 60–106 in (1.5–2.7 m)
HEIGHT: 26–32 in (66–81 cm)

The powerful and majestic mountain lion is the largest and most secretive cat of the Rockies. Seldom seen by people, mountain lions are becoming increasingly threatened by human encroachment and development, habitat loss, and trophy hunting. Their coat is tawny to grayish-brown. They feed primarily on mule deer and elk, often sitting in trees above animal trails waiting to pounce on prey. Like domestic cats, they groom themselves frequently, but they have a much louder purr! **Where found:** in a wide range of habitats from low-elevation valleys and foothills to tree-line; throughout the Rockies. **Also known as:** cougar, puma, catamount, panther.

Lynx
Lynx canadensis

LENGTH: 30–43 in (76–110 cm)
HEIGHT: 18–23 in (46–58 cm)

With long legs and huge, snowshoe-like paws, the lynx is uniquely adapted for catching snowshoe hares on snow, so much so that cyclical increases and decreases in hare populations cause lynx populations to follow similar trends. Lynx are shy and seldom seen, but these beautiful cats are important members of the forest community. The facial ruff, long black ear tufts and completely black-tipped short tail are distinctive features. The coat is gray to orange-brown. **Where found:** dense old-growth coniferous forests with heavy undergrowth; throughout the Canadian Rockies but restricted to high-elevation mountains in Montana, Idaho, Wyoming, and Colorado.

Bobcat

Lynx rufus

LENGTH: 30–48 in (76–122 cm)
HEIGHT: 17–20 in (43–50 cm)

The nocturnal bobcat is the smallest of the Rocky Mountain wild cats. It feeds on a wide range of prey, including rabbits, voles, mice, birds, reptiles, and insects. It is highly adaptable in its use of habitats, and may be seen close to residential areas. Like most young cats, bobcat kittens are almost always at play. **Where found:** in most habitats that provide some type of woody cover; common throughout the U.S. Rockies, but restricted to southern areas of the Canadian Rockies.

Ringtail

Bassariscus astutus

LENGTH: 25–32 in (64–81 cm)

The ringtail is a seldom seen, nocturnal omnivore. It is a skillful mouser that usually lives close to water. It dens in hollow trees, rock piles, crevices, caves, and occasionally unused buildings. Its long, ringed tail is as long as its body, which is built like a that of a small housecat. **Where found:** dry forests and rocky areas close to water; up to 9200 ft (2804 m); Colorado, Utah, and New Mexico. **Also known as:** cacomistle, civet cat, miner's cat.

Raccoon

Procyon lotor

LENGTH: 25–37 in (64–94 cm)

Raccoons are highly intelligent and dexterous omnivores, currently expanding their range west into the foothills of the Rockies. They are excellent climbers, active primarily at night. Human food and garbage containers are no match for the raccoon's curiosity, persistence, and problem-solving abilities. It has a long, grizzled, gray to reddish-brown coat and is similar in size to a large, fat housecat. **Where found:** lower-elevation riparian areas, shorelines, campgrounds, townsites, fields, and forested areas near water; southern B.C. and Alberta south.

Wolverine
Gulo gulo
LENGTH: 30–43 in (76–110 cm)

Largest of the Rocky Mountain weasels, the wolverine looks like a small, frazzled bear. As an omnivorous scavenger it is an ecologically valuable inhabitant of true wilderness. Unfortunately, it has a poor reputation owing to its occasional habit of raiding unoccupied wilderness cabins. After eating the edible contents, it tends to spray any leftovers with a foul-smelling musk from its anal musk gland...plenty of incentive to lock your cabin tight! **Where found:** near treeline and on alpine tundra; B.C., Alberta, Montana, Idaho, and Colorado. **Also known as:** glutton, skunk bear.

Badger
Taxidea taxus
LENGTH: 25–35 in (64–89 cm)

Equipped with huge claws and strong forelimbs, the badger can dig a hole almost as fast as the eye can blink. Its powerful jaws, long teeth, and aggressive defense tactics make it a formidable fighter against most predators. The badger has short legs and a squat, shaggy body. Badgers have been known to hunt cooperatively with coyotes. Badger holes are essential in providing homes for many burrowing creatures. **Where found:** low-elevation fields, meadows, grasslands, fencelines, and ditches; throughout the Rockies.

Northern River Otter
Lutra canadensis
LENGTH: 35–55 in (90–140 cm)

If you have met a frisky family of otters, you will never forget their playful aquatic antics and games. Their fully webbed feet, long, streamlined body, and muscular tail make them swift swimmers with incredible fishing ability. River otters are highly social animals, usually traveling in small groups. Listen for their grunting vocalizations and look for their 'slides' on the shores of waterbodies. **Where found:** near lakes, ponds, and streams; throughout the Rockies.

Fisher

Martes pennanti

LENGTH: 31–42 in (79–107 cm)

Fishers are the size of a small fox. They will eat any animal they can overpower, but are distinguished along with mountain lions for their ability to prey upon large numbers of porcupines. Amazingly, they possess this skill without the guidance and teachings of their parents. **Where found:** dense mixed and coniferous forests; avoids open areas; B.C. and Alberta to Wyoming and Utah.

Marten

Martes americana

LENGTH: 22–26 in (56–66 cm)

An expert climber with semi-retractable claws, this forest dweller is quick and agile enough to catch arboreal squirrels such as the red squirrel. Although it spends most of its time on the ground, the marten often dens in a tree-hollow, where it raises its annual litter of 1–5 kits. Martens have a light reddish-brown to dark brown body and bushy tail with a distinctive yellow-orange chest and throat patch. Its legs and tail are darker than its head and body. **Where found:** old-growth coniferous forests of spruce and fir; throughout the Rockies. **Also known as:** American sable.

Mink

Mustela vison

LENGTH: 17–25 in (43–64 cm)

The mink is most often seen hunting along shorelines. Its partially webbed feet make it an excellent swimmer and diver, and it often finds its food underwater. Its thick, dark brown to blackish, oily fur insulates the body from extremely cold waters. Mink travel along established hunting routes, sometimes resting in a muskrat lodge after eating the original inhabitant. **Where found:** shorelines of lakes, marshes, and streams; throughout the Rockies.

Long-tailed Weasel
Mustela frenata
LENGTH: 12–18 in (30–46 cm)

This weasel has adapted to a variety of wild and rural habitats. It feeds on small rodents, birds, insects, reptiles, amphibians, and occasionally fruits and berries. It will even prey on species twice its size, including rabbits, muskrats, and ground squirrels. Like other true weasels, it turns white in winter but the tip of the tail remains black. **Where found:** grassy meadows, brushland, woodlots, forest edges, and fencerows; common throughout the Rockies.

Short-tailed Weasel
Mustela erminea
LENGTH: 10–13 in (25–33 cm)

A common inhabitant of subalpine meadows and forests, the short-tailed weasel is a voracious nocturnal hunter. A spontaneous encounter with this curious creature will reveal its extraordinary speed and agility. Mice and voles form the bulk of this weasel's diet. Its coat is white in winter but the tail is black-tipped year-round. **Where found:** dense, mixed, and coniferous forests to shrublands, lakeshores, riparian areas, meadows, and alpine tundra; throughout the Rockies. **Also known as:** ermine, stoat.

Least Weasel
Mustela nivalis
LENGTH: 6½–8½ in (16.5–21.5 cm)

Although it weighs less than a pika (p. 43), the least weasel is a formidable predator of small rodents, amphibians, and insects. Its tiny, thin body allows it to race after voles and mice in their own underground tunnels and dens. The high metabolic rate of the least weasel is as high as some shrews, demanding near-constant input of food. This weasel turns all white in winter. **Where found:** woodlots, fencerows, fields, meadows, shrublands, riparian areas, and mixed forests; most likely to be found in the Northern U.S. and Canadian Rockies.

Striped Skunk
Mephitis mephitis
LENGTH: 21–30 in (53–76 cm)

Many people are familiar with the distinct smell of our most common skunk, but few have enjoyed watching one going about its business. A true omnivore and mainly nocturnal, this skunk eats voles, insects, worms, berries, nuts, leaves, and eggs among other things. It uses its odorous musk gland to mark its territory and to repel danger. Watching skunks is great fun—just make sure you keep at least 20 ft (6 m) away!

Where found: most lower-elevation habitats; throughout the Rockies.

Western Spotted Skunk
Spilogale gracilis
LENGTH: 8–13 in (20–33 cm)

This nocturnal member of the Weasel Family is adept at climbing trees. When threatened, it stamps its feet in alarm or makes short lunges at the source of danger. If such warnings go unheeded, it assumes a handstand position and walks toward its target, arching its back and flipping its tail down toward its head, allowing it to spray its assailant. **Where found:** lower-elevation riparian areas, open forests, grasslands, canyons, and brushlands; Idaho and Montana south.

Black-tailed Jackrabbit

Lepus californicus

LENGTH: 16–25 in (41–64 cm)

This hare can often be seen at dawn and dusk grazing at roadsides. Large, black-tipped ears detect danger and release excess body heat on hot summer days. Although it can run up to 35 mph (55 km/h) and leap 20 ft (6 m) when frightened, the black-tailed jackrabbit still falls prey to eagles, hawks, owls, coyotes, and bobcats. It does not turn white in winter. **Where found:** lower-elevation shrublands, sagebrush, fields, and grasslands in foothills; from Idaho, Utah, and Colorado south.

White-tailed Jackrabbit

Lepus townsendii

LENGTH: 19–28 in (49.5–70 cm)

Unlike rabbits, which give birth to altricial young and hide from danger, hares give birth to precocial young and try to outrun predators. This hare is capable of running 45 mph (72 km/h) in short spurts. Before taking flight, it sits motionless with its ears laid flat over its back. Its buffy to brownish-gray pelage turns white in winter. Its undersides, hind feet, and tail remain white and the long ears remain black-tipped year-round. **Where found:** grasslands, shrublands, and sagebrush; from southern Alberta south, except for a population gap in southeastern B.C., northern Idaho, and northwestern Montana.

Snowshoe Hare

Lepus americanus

LENGTH: 14–20 in (35.5–52 cm)

This primarily nocturnal hare camouflages seasonally: it has a grayish, reddish, or blackish-brown pelage in summer and white pelage in winter (the ears remain black-tipped and the tail and belly remain white year-round). This adaptation helps a motionless hare avoid predators including the agile lynx. If detected, the hare explodes into a running zig-zag pattern in its flight for cover, reaching speeds of up to 32 mph (50 km/h) on hard-packed snow trails. Hare populations rise and fall in a cyclical relationship with lynx. **Where found:** brushy, second-growth forests up to treeline; throughout the Rockies. **Also known as:** varying hare.

Mountain Cottontail
Sylvilagus nuttallii
LENGTH: 14–18 in (36–46 cm)

Generally active from dusk until dawn, the mountain cottontail occasionally rests in the shade of a shrub during the day. Because cottontails burrow, they must endure the company of parasites including ticks, whose swollen, grape-like bodies cling to the cottontail's ears. Cottontails are born blind and naked. Adults do not camouflage in winter, but remain gray with a rusty-brown nape of neck and black-tipped ears. The belly and underside of the tail are white. **Where found:** sagebrush, rocky areas interspersed with shrubs and riparian areas; from southern Montana and Idaho south. **Also known as:** Nuttall's cottontail.

Pika
Ochotona princeps
LENGTH: 7–8 in (18–20 cm)

This busy creature scurries in and out of rocky crevices to issue its warning *PEEEK!* call and to gather succulent grasses. These grasses are dried in mounds on sun-drenched rocks, to be stored for later consumption during winter. Although it looks like a rodent, this rambunctious, spirited creature is more closely related to rabbits and hares. The tailless pika has a grayish, reddish, or blackish-brown coat with gray undersides. **Where found:** rocky talus slopes and rocky fields at higher elevations; throughout the Rockies. **Also known as:** cony.

Porcupine
Erethizon dorsatum
LENGTH: 26–41 in (66–104 cm)

Contrary to popular myth, porcupines cannot throw their 30,000 or so quills, but they do rely on a lightning-fast flick of the tail to deliver the quills into persistent attackers. Porcupines are excellent tree climbers that feed on forbs, shrubs, and the sugary cambium layer of trees. Their insatiable craving for salt occasionally drives them to gnaw on rubber tires, wooden ax handles, toilet seats, and even hiking boots! **Where found:** coniferous and mixed deciduous-coniferous forests up to the subalpine; throughout the Rockies.

Beaver
Castor canadensis
LENGTH: 36–48 in (91–122 cm)

The loud slap of a beaver's tail on water warns of intruders. Beavers are skillful and unrelenting in the construction and maintenance of their dams and lodges. Shrubs and fallen trees serve as both food and building materials. Beavers' long, continuously growing front incisors are perfect tools for gnawing down trees. Beavers can remain submerged under water for up to 15 minutes. Their broad, flattened tail is an extremely effective propulsion device. **Where found:** lakes, ponds, marshes, and slow-flowing rivers and streams at most elevations; throughout the Rockies.

Muskrat
Ondatra zibethica
LENGTH: 19–24 in (48–61 cm)

Considered to be a giant vole, the muskrat is an important aquatic creature in freshwater environments. The muskrat's construction of open-water canals and floating houses of aquatic vegetation creates habitats for many species of waterfowl and aquatic plants that could not otherwise survive in dense stands of cattails and sedges. Muskrats feed heavily on cattails, but will also eat a variety of other plants and animals. The pelage is silvery or reddish-brown to blackish. The tail is narrow and flattened. **Where found:** lakes, marshes, ponds, rivers, reservoirs, dugouts, and canals; throughout the Rockies.

Hoary Marmot
Marmota caligata
LENGTH: 27–30 in (69–75 cm)

When all else fails...sleep! That's the hoary marmot's strategy for surviving in its harsh, high alpine environment. A marmot hibernates 5–9 months each year from October to February in the U.S. Rockies and from September to May in the Canadian Rockies. It requires the entire summer to build up its fat reserves by eating alpine plants. This marmot has few predators but will fall prey to golden eagles, grizzlies, and wolverines. **Where found:** rocky subalpine slopes, rock slides, and alpine meadows; Alberta, B.C., Idaho, and Montana. **Also known as:** mountain marmot, whistler, rockchuck.

Yellow-bellied Marmot
Marmota flaviventris
LENGTH: 19–26 in (47–66 cm)

Yellow-bellied marmots excavate a network of burrows under the rocky terrain to find shelter from freezing temperatures, strong winds, golden eagles, mountain lions, and grizzly bears. These marmots live in harem colonies and bask in the sun on warm summer days. Look for the dark head with the yellowish band across the bridge of nose. **Where found:** rocky subalpine slopes and outcroppings close to a source of grassy or herbaceous vegetation; from extreme southern B.C. and Alberta south. **Also known as:** yellow-footed marmot.

Northern Flying Squirrel
Glaucomys sabrinus
LENGTH: 9½–14 in (24–36 cm)

Long flaps of skin stretched between the fore and hind limbs (called the 'patagium') and a broad, flattened tail allow the nocturnal northern flying squirrel to glide swiftly from tree to tree. After emerging from its tree cavity nest, it floats down to the forest floor where it feeds on a variety of food, including mycorhizal fungi. Through its stool, the squirrel spreads the beneficial fungus, helping both the fungus and the forest plants. **Where found:** primarily old-growth coniferous and mixed forests; from B.C. and Alberta to Wyoming and Utah.

Abert's Squirrel
Sciurus aberti
LENGTH: 18–23 in (46.5–58 cm)

This handsome tree squirrel builds an elaborate all-season nest in the crotch of a ponderosa pine, where it raises young and finds shelter during cold or wet weather. From March to April, females entice several males to engage in a 'chase' through the trees before selecting a mate. Arizona populations of this species separated by the Grand Canyon show different color variations. The long, bushy tail is outlined in white, with whitish undersides, and the long, tasseled ears have reddish-brown backs. **Where found:** ponderosa pine and piñon-juniper forests; Colorado and New Mexico. **Also known as:** tasssel-eared squirrel.

Red Squirrel
Tamiasciurus hudsonicus
LENGTH: 11–13½ in (28–34 cm)

Intruders beware! This fearless and extremely vocal tree squirrel may chatter, stomp its feet, flick its tail and scold you with a piercing cry until you flee from its territory. The large middens of discarded pinecone scales are evidence of its buried bounty of food. A more patient squirrel allows you to watch it feed on pinecones like corn-on-the-cob. The short pelage is rusty-red to olive-brown with a white undertail. **Where found:** coniferous and mixed forests at various elevations; throughout the Rockies. **Also known as:** pine squirrel, chickaree.

Rock Squirrel
Spermophilus variegatus
LENGTH: 17–21 in (43–53 cm)

If there are rocks nearby, they are probably home to a colony of rock squirrels. Primarily crepuscular in their activities, they eat and store a wide variety of seeds, fruits, nuts, and plants. Females form maternal groups around main burrowing sites. These colonies are aggressively defended by adult males. **Where found:** rocky canyons, cliffs, talus slopes, boulder fields, and roadside slopes; Utah, Colorado, and New Mexico.

Wyoming Ground Squirrel
Spermophilus elegans
LENGTH: 10–12 in (25–31 cm)

Stiff competition for food means that the omnivorous Wyoming ground squirrel will even cannibalize the remains of its own kind killed by vehicles. Vital nutrients and energy thus remain within the species in the unrelenting struggle for survival. Once considered to be a form of the more northerly Richardson's ground squirrel (*S. richardsonii*), the Wyoming is now identified by taxonomists as a separate species. **Where found:** sagebrush, montane grassland, and talus slopes; southern Wyoming to northern Colorado, and eastern Idaho to southwestern Montana.

Columbian Ground Squirrel
Spermophilus columbianus
LENGTH: 13–15 in (33–38 cm)

The Columbian ground squirrel is a commonly seen diurnal omnivore. It eats a variety of foods including herbaceous plants, grasses, insects, birds, eggs, and even smaller vertebrates. Like other ground squirrels, it hibernates in winter and estivates (a dormant state similar to hibernation) during hot, dry spells to conserve energy. **Where found:** sagebrush, fields, and montane meadows at mid- to high elevations; B.C., Alberta, Idaho, and Montana.

Uinta Ground Squirrel
Spermophilus armatus
LENGTH: 11–12 in (28–31 cm)

This squirrel occupies an ecological niche similar to that of the Columbian ground squirrel to the north, but it is more similar to the Richardson's ground squirrel (*S. richardsonii*) of the prairies (the Uinta is distinguished by its light-tipped, dark tail hairs). When ground squirrels emerge from underground hibernation in spring, they provide easy prey for coyotes, badgers, and migrating hawks. Their omniverous diet includes seeds, insects, forbs, and some small vertebrates. **Where found:** sagebrush-grasslands, field edges, and subalpine meadows; southwestern Montana, southeastern Idaho, northeastern Utah, and western Wyoming.

Golden-mantled Ground Squirrel
Spermophilus lateralis
LENGTH: 10½–13 in (27–32 cm)

These high elevation ground squirrels have chipmunk-like markings and omnivorous diets. They are diurnal, but remain in their burrows during bouts of inclement weather. Much of summer is spent foraging, sunbathing, retreating to their burrows for midday siestas or inadvertently entertaining us. Notice the 2 broad, white stripes extending down the back from the neck (not from the head like chipmunks), bordered by black stripes. **Where found:** open coniferous forests on mountain and foothills slopes up to alpine tundra; throughout the Rockies. **Also known as:** copperhead.

White-tailed Prairie Dog

Cynomys leucurus

LENGTH: 13–15 in (34–37 cm)

Prairie dogs are highly social, diurnal rodents that form large burrowing colonies. Sentry guards scrutinize the surrounding land and enveloping sky for signs of danger and intrusion, while the rest of the colony continues to forage, sunbathe, groom, and play. A series of loud yaps warning of danger causes the entire colony to vanish underground. Prairie dogs occasionally share their dens with western rattlesnakes, Great Basin gopher snakes, and burrowing owls (*Athene cunicularia*). **Where found:** dry mountain valleys and sagebrush-grasslands at high elevations; Wyoming, Utah, and Colorado.

Red-tailed Chipmunk

Tamias ruficaudus

Length: 8¾–10 in (22–25 cm)

The most arboreal (tree-dwelling) of the chipmunks, this species builds well-insulated ball-shaped nests in trees or on the ground using dried grasses. It defends its territory with a warning bark. When it is not defending its territory or hiding from predators, it collects, caches, and eats seeds or often preforms charming sun- and soil-bathing antics. It is similar to least (p. 49) and yellow-pine chipmunks (below) with the exception of a grayish back and belly, dark gray rump, rufous shoulders and sides, and a bright orange or rust-colored underside of the tail. **Where found:** dense, subalpine spruce-fir forests: B.C., Montana, northern Idaho, and extreme southwestern Alberta.

Yellow-pine Chipmunk

Tamias amoenus

LENGTH: 8¼–9⅛ in (21–23 cm)

Flowing bushy tails, striped faces and backs, bursting round cheeks filled with seeds, and dashes in and out of rocks and vegetation all characterize these endearing Rocky Mountain chipmunks. Distinct dorsal stripes alternate: 5 dark and 4 light. On the face, look for 3 dark stripes on each cheek with the middle stripe through the eye. Watch for yellow-pine chipmunks in open forests of…yellow pines (ponderosa pine)! **Where found:** open coniferous and montane forests, forest edges, and burned sites up to treeline; B.C., Alberta, Idaho, Montana, and Wyoming.

Colorado Chipmunk
Tamias quadrivittatus
LENGTH: 8–9½ in (20–24 cm)

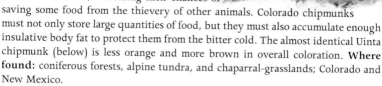

Chipmunks tend to scatter their food among several cache sites, increasing their chances of saving some food from the thievery of other animals. Colorado chipmunks must not only store large quantities of food, but they must also accumulate enough insulative body fat to protect them from the bitter cold. The almost identical Uinta chipmunk (below) is less orange and more brown in overall coloration. **Where found:** coniferous forests, alpine tundra, and chaparral-grasslands; Colorado and New Mexico.

Uinta Chipmunk
Tamias umbrinus
LENGTH: 8–9½ in (20–24 cm)

The Uinta chipmunk is virtually identical to the Colorado chipmunk (above) but with a black-tipped tail bordered with white. This tree-dwelling chipmunk can be found in high elevation habitats similar to those occupied by the red-tailed chipmunk further north. It prefers mature lodgepole pine stands with an open understory and rocky ground surface. It is typically solitary and relatively silent. **Where found:** subalpine coniferous forests and rocky slopes up to treeline; east-central Idaho, northwestern Wyoming, northeastern Utah, and north-central Colorado.

Least Chipmunk
Tamias minimus
LENGTH: 6¾–9 in (17–23 cm)

This cute and curious rodent is the smallest of our chipmunks. The many western chipmunk species can be difficult to tell apart, but populations are separated by different habitat preferences. Least chipmunks are highly adaptable and will live just about any place not already occupied by another species of chipmunk. They are identified by the gray belly and nape of neck, and 5 brown-edged dorsal stripes with 2 extending onto the head. The tail is pale orange underneath. **Where found:** sagebrush, campgrounds, coniferous forests, and alpine areas; Alberta, B.C., northern Montana, and from southern Idaho south.

Southern Red-backed Vole

Clethrionomys gapperi

LENGTH: 4¾–6½ in (12–17 cm)

Active by day in higher elevation spruce-fir forests and bogs, this vole is easily recognized by its reddish-brown back on an otherwise grayish body. Like other voles, it does not hibernate during winter; instead, it tunnels around the subnivean layer—along the ground, under the snow—in search of seeds, nuts, and leaves. Voles are extremely prolific but populations will vary according to predator populations and available food supplies. **Where found:** mixed-wood and coniferous forests, bogs, and riparian areas; throughout the Rockies.

Heather Vole

Phenacomys intermedius

LENGTH: 4¾–6 in (12–15 cm)

Rarely seen because of their nocturnal habits, heather voles enjoy a summer diet of grasses, bark, leaves, lichen, seeds, fungi, and berries. In winter, they create subnivean food caches near their nesting sites by collecting bark from shrubs and leaves from evergreen plants. Gnaw marks at the bottom of willow or birch provide evidence of their presence. Dark brown to grayish-brown pelage and silvery undersides with white feet and a bi-colored tail mark this vole. **Where found:** coniferous forests, mountain meadows, and talus slopes with evergreen herbs and shrubs; from B.C. and Alberta south. **Also known as:** mountain phenacomys.

Long-tailed Vole

Microtus longicaudus

LENGTH: 6–7½ in (15–19 cm)

Long-tailed voles are found only in the mountainous areas of western North America, and are essential members of the Rocky Mountain food web. They eat a variety of plants, fungi, and invertebrates. Healthy vole populations support many predator species of mammals, birds, and reptiles. This dark gray to brown vole has gray undersides and a long, bi-colored tail. **Where found:** mountain meadows and riparian areas; throughout the Rockies.

Montane Vole

Microtus montanus

LENGTH: 5–7 in (13–18 cm)

As with most voles, the montane vole is distinguished from mice by its small, rounded ears and relatively short tail. It has a grizzled brown to gray pelage with light gray to white undersides. This vole shares many habits and habitat preferences with the more widely distributed meadow vole, but it is rarely found where the meadow vole is established. Favorable environmental conditions may allow montane voles to reproduce to brief densities of 10,000 to 30,000 voles per hectare! **Where found:** a variety of habitats at various elevations, usually wherever the meadow vole is absent; Montana and Idaho south. **Also known as:** mountain vole, Montana vole.

Meadow Vole

Microtus pennsylvanicus

LENGTH: 5 1/2–8 in (14–20 cm)

A complex network of grass-covered runways remaining on a meadow surface after the spring thaw is evidence of the busy meadow vole. Primarily active at night, this common vole can occasionally be seen in the daytime along fencelines, in agricultural fields, and on urban meadows. As a response to high predation rates, meadow voles are ready to breed 3–4 weeks after birth. The pelage is brown to blackish-brown with gray undersides. **Where found:** lower-elevation meadows, open woodlands, orchards, agricultural fields, fencelines, and marshes; throughout the Rockies. **Also known as:** fieldmouse.

Water Vole

Microtus richardsoni

LENGTH: 9–11 in (23–28 cm)

An excellent swimmer and diver, the water vole lives along streams. Its dense, water-repellent underfur insulates its body from the cold water. To avoid predators, it builds extensive networks of burrows, often with direct entrances into water. However, few water voles live beyond 1 year, falling prey to weasels, hawks, owls, snakes, and foxes. It is a very large, blackish-brown vole with gray sides and grayish-white undersides, long hind feet and an indistinctly bi-colored tail. **Where found:** high-elevation riparian areas and meadows; from B.C. and Alberta to Wyoming and Utah. **Also known as:** Richardson's water vole.

Northern Pocket Gopher

Thomomys talpoides

LENGTH: 7^1/$_2$–10 in (19–25.5 cm)

The northern pocket gopher is a supremely adapted subterranean rodent. The soles of its naked feet are equipped with long front claws for digging. Furred lips that extend over the long incisor teeth prevent dirt from entering the mouth while eating and digging, and fur-lined cheek pouches temporarily store succulent roots, tubers, and green plants. Although it spends most of its life underground, it occasionally tunnels to the surface at night to find lush herbaceous plants, leaving dirt mounds at the surface. **Where found:** mountain meadows, fields, shrublands, grasslands, and open pine forests; from extreme southern B.C. and Alberta south.

Bushy-tailed Woodrat

Neotoma cinerea

LENGTH: 15–17 in (38–43 cm)

This curious, nocturnal rodent is infamous for its collection of natural and man-made objects, including twigs, bones, pinecones, bottle caps, rings, pens, and coins—often trading an object in its mouth for a more attractive item. The woodrat incorporates these objects into its massive nest, usually tucked into a crevice, under a rock pile, or in a tree. Urine-stained rocks or a permanent musky smell indicate the presence of this busy creature. This tawny-gray to blackish rodent has white undersides and a diagnostic bushy, squirrel-like tail. **Where found:** talus slopes, caves, crevices, and rocky outcroppings in coniferous forests; throughout the Rockies. **Also known as:** packrat.

Northern Bog Lemming

Synaptomys borealis

LENGTH: 4^3/$_4$–5^1/$_2$ in (12–14 cm)

A fleeting view of a brown ball of fur racing through the hummocky ground of a sphagnum bog may be your only sight of this busy rodent. The northern bog lemming maintains an extensive network of mossy runways year-round, and feeds mainly on sedges and grasses. Like most other small mammals, this lemming remains active throughout winter and is an important source of food for many predators. **Where found:** wet alpine tundra, lake borders, sphagnum bogs, and black spruce forests with Labrador tea and moss; B.C., Alberta, and extreme northern Montana and Idaho.

Western Harvest Mouse
Reithrodontomys megalotis
LENGTH: 4³/₄–6 in (12–15 cm)

The harvest mouse is named for its habit of collecting grasses in mounds along its network of trails.
Ball-shaped nests are woven from grass and lined with
soft plant down. Amazingly, females may produce up to 14
litters in a single year, each averaging 4 young per litter!
The short gray to brown pelage with white to gray under-
sides has a diagnostic dark band down the length of the back and a bi-colored tail.
Where found: grasslands, meadows, fields, fencelines, and riparian areas with
scattered shrubs and forbs; eastern Idaho, eastern Utah, southern Colorado, and
New Mexico.

Deer Mouse
Peromyscus maniculatus
LENGTH: 4³/₄–7 in (12–18 cm)

The abundant deer mouse is a seed eater, but it
will eat insects, spiders, caterpillars, fungi,
flowers, berries, and even some bird eggs. Unlike
most mammals, the male deer mouse often helps the female
raise their young. Deer mice are great climbers and sources of food for many
other animals. Less than 5 percent of wild deer mice live for a complete year.
Deer mice have a distinctly bi-colored tail, a grayish, reddish, or tawny brown coat
with white undersides and feet. **Where found:** most dry habitats; throughout the
Rockies.

House Mouse
Mus musculus
LENGTH: 5¹/₂–7¹/₂ in (14–19 cm)

This familiar mouse can be found
throughout most of North America.
Like the Norway rat it arrived as a stow-
away on ships from Europe, quickly
spreading across the continent alongside
European settlers. It is nocturnal in habit, and
may be responsible for gnawing the labels off the canned soup stored in your
cupboards! Its pelage is brownish to blackish-gray with gray undersides.
Where found: usually associated with human settlements, including urban houses,
garages, farmyards, garbage dumps, and granaries; throughout the Rockies.

Norway Rat
Rattus norvegicus
LENGTH: 12–18 in (30–46 cm)

Native to Europe and Asia, the Norway rat came to North America as a stow-away on early ships. It mainly associates with human settlements, feeding on cereal grains, fruits, vegetation, and garbage. Norway rats can carry parasites and diseases that are transferable to wildlife, humans, and pets, but captive bred rats have given psychologists many insights into human learning and behavior. Wild Norway rats have brown to reddish-brown, often grizzled pelage with gray tones and gray undersides. **Where found:** urban areas, farmyards, and garbage dumps; throughout much of the Rockies. **Also known as:** brown rat, common rat, sewer rat, water rat.

Ord's Kangaroo Rat
Dipodomys ordii
LENGTH: 10–11 in (25–28 cm)

Powerful hind legs and a long, muscular tail give this endearing little creature the ability to leap 6–8 ft (1.8–2.5 m) in a single hop. Mainly a nocturnal granivore, it forages for seeds and the occasional plant or insect by night, while resting in its short, sandy burrow by day. It rarely drinks water, obtaining needed liquids from food and internally recycled wastes. **Where found:** grasslands, shrublands, sand dunes, and open areas with sandy soils; Wyoming, Utah, Colorado, and New Mexico.

Western Jumping Mouse
Zapus princeps
LENGTH: 7–9 in (18–23 cm)

This mouse is a great digger, swimmer, and jumper. When startled by danger, it uses its large back legs and long tail to jump over 6 ft (1.8 m) to safer ground. It is usually active at night, foraging for seeds and the occasional insect. Before hibernating, this mouse will nearly double its weight, then snuggle up in a ball of grass at the back of a burrow. The pelage varies from a dark to olive-brown back, orange to pale yellow sides, and with buffy white underparts. **Where found:** damp meadows, especially along streambanks and marshes; throughout the Rockies.

Water Shrew
Sorex palustris
LENGTH: 5–6½ in (13–17 cm)

Large hind feet fitted with stiff, bristly
hairs, and thick body fur that insulates
by trapping air bubbles between the
hairs, allow the water shrew to hunt aquatic invertebrates in cold ponds and
streams. Its larger size and specialized aquatic adaptations also allow it to catch and
eat small fish and tadpoles that other shrews cannot. The coat is dark velvety brown
to black with whitish-gray undersides and a distinct bi-colored tail. **Where found:**
lakes, ponds, marshes, and streams with vegetated shorelines; throughout the
Rockies. **Also known as:** northern water shrew.

Dusky Shrew
Sorex monticolus
LENGTH: 3¾–5 ½ in (9–14 cm)

Shrews have an incredibly high metabolic
rate, with heart rates often reaching 1200
beats per minute! Most of the heat energy
they produce is quickly lost to the environment,
and so shrews must eat their own body weight of
food each day to maintain their internal body temperature.
Dusky shrews who go without food for more than a few hours will starve to death.
This shrew has a brown back and sides, but is gray underneath with an overall
darker pelage in winter. **Where found:** wide variety of wet to moist habitats;
throughout the Rockies. **Also known as:** montane shrew.

Pygmy Shrew
Sorex hoyi
LENGTH: 2¾–4 in (7–10 cm)

The pygmy shrew is the smallest
mammal of the 'New World.' It is
distinguished from other shrews by
its tiny size and a tail that is usually less than
40 percent of the shrew's total length. Look for its long, constantly twitching
snout as it hunts for insects and carrion, and keep your nose tuned for their strong
musk odor. Pygmy shrews may consume more than three times their own body
weight in food each day to survive. All shrews are insectivores. **Where found:**
spruce-fir forests, bogs, and wetlands; B.C., Alberta, northern Montana, and
northern Idaho.

Western Long-eared Myotis
Myotis evotis
LENGTH: 3½–4 in (9–10 cm)
WINGSPAN: 10⅝ in (27 cm)

Like all other Rocky Mountain bats, this bat uses echolocation to navigate and find prey in complete darkness. By producing short bursts of high frequency sound, then listening for the echo bouncing off objects in the distance, bats can determine the direction, distance, size, and texture of objects to avoid or eat. The long, black ears are ¾ in (2 cm) with a long, sharp tragus. **Where found:** roosts in buildings, under tree bark, and occasionally in caves; hibernates in caves and mine adits; in many habitats at various elevations; throughout the Rockies.

Little Brown Myotis
Myotis lucifugus
LENGTH: 3–4 in (8–10 cm)
WINGSPAN: 9¾ in (25 cm)

These common bats form large maternal roosting colonies each summer to give birth and raise young. Virtually helpless at birth, a single offspring spends its first few days clinging to the chest of its mother until it is strong enough to remain at the roost site. The ears are ½ in (13 mm) with a blunt tragus half as long as the ear. The Yuma myotis (*Myotis yumanensis*) is virtually identical but also has a more southern range in the Rockies. **Where found:** roosts in buildings, barns, caves, rock crevices, hollow trees, and under tree bark; hibernates in buildings, caves, and mine adits; in many habitats at various elevations; throughout the Rockies. **Also known as:** little brown bat.

Hoary Bat
Lasiurus cinereus
LENGTH: 4¾–5½ in (12–14 cm)
WINGSPAN: 15 in (39 cm)

This beautiful bat is an odd-ball among its kind—both males and females live solitary lives, with females usually giving birth to 2 young. They roost in trees, not caves or buildings, and wrap their wings around themselves for protection against the elements. Hoary bats often roost in orchards, but they are insectivores and do not damage fruit crops. At night, look for their large size and slow wingbeats over open terrain. **Where found:** roosts on the branches of coniferous and deciduous trees and occasionally in tree cavities; throughout the Rockies.

Silver-haired Bat
Lasionycteris noctivagans
LENGTH: 3½–4½ in (9–11 cm)
WINGSPAN: 12 in (30 cm)

The silver-haired bat is similar to the hoary bat in its habit of roosting in trees, but it can be found in small, loose groups. It takes flight about half an hour after sunset to patrol open fields, water surfaces, or treetops for prey. To conserve energy on cold days, it can lower its body temperature and metabolism—a state known as 'torpor.' The black flight membrane spans 12 in (30 cm). **Where found:** roosts in cavities and crevices of old-growth trees; throughout the Rockies.

Big Brown Bat
Eptesicus fuscus
LENGTH: 4–5 in (10–13 cm)
WINGSPAN: 13 in (33 cm)

An effective aerial hunter, the big brown bat's ultrasonic echolocation (80,000 to 40,000 hertz) can detect flying beetles and moths up to 16½ ft (5 m) away. It flies above water or around street lights searching for prey, which it scoops up with its wing and tail membranes. **Where found:** common in and around man-made structures, occasionally roosting in hollow trees and rock crevices; throughout the Rockies.

Townsend's Big-eared Bat
Plecotus townsendii
LENGTH: 3–4⅜ in (8–11 cm)
WINGSPAN: 11 in (28.5 cm)

Endowed with relatively enormous ears, these bats catch night-flying moths and flying insects. Bats often hunt for brief periods (10–20 minutes) to fill their stomachs before finding a comfortable night roost. After digesting their first meal, they alight again to hunt. Townsend's big-eared bats, like most bats, are extremely sensitive to disturbance during winter hibernation. Their ears are half the entire body length, with a long, sharp tragus. **Where found:** caves, buildings, or old mines; throughout the U.S. Rockies and extreme southern B.C. **Also known as:** western big-eared bat.

GUIDE TO THE BIRD GROUPS

DIVING BIRDS
pp. 59–60

HERON & CRANE
pp. 60–61

RAIL & COOT
p. 61

WATERFOWL
pp. 62–65

BIRDS OF PREY
pp. 66–69

GROUSE & PTARMIGAN
p. 69

SHOREBIRDS,
GULL & TERN, pp. 70–71

DOVES
p. 71

WOODPECKERS
pp. 72–73

NIGHTHAWK
& KINGFISHER
p. 74

HUMMINGBIRDS
p. 75

FLYCATCHERS, SWIFT
& SWALLOWS
pp. 76–77

CORVIDS
pp. 78–79

SMALL SONGBIRDS
pp. 80–83

BLUEBIRD, THRUSHES &
VIREO
pp. 84–85

TANAGER &
WARBLERS
pp. 85–87

LARK, STARLING &
SHRIKE
p. 88

CATBIRD, WAXWING
& DIPPER
p. 89

SPARROWS
pp. 90–91

BLACKBIRDS,
MEADOWLARKS & ORIOLE
pp. 92–93

FINCH-LIKE
BIRDS
pp. 93–95

BIRDS

Birds are all feathered but not all fly and they lay hard-shelled eggs. Some birds migrate south in the colder winter months and return north in spring. For this reason the Rocky Mountains have a different diversity of birds in summer than in winter. Many migrating Rocky Mountain birds fly as far south as Central and South America. These neotropical migrants have concerned biologists and conservationists because pesticide use and decreased habitat in these countries threaten the survival of many species. Appreciation for wildlife may encourage solutions to this problem. Birdwatching is a popular activity with many visitors to the Rocky Mountains.

Common Loon

Gavia immer

LENGTH: 31–35 in (79–89 cm)

The haunting wails, spirited tremolo, and piercing yodels of the enchanting loon embrace all listeners. Dense, marrow-filled bones, the ability to quickly expel air from its feathers, and internal air sacs make the loon an effective diver and swimmer. However, heavy bones and relatively small wings force the loon to run on the water surface for long distances before becoming airborne. Fortunate observers may see the iridescent green and pink of the loon's otherwise blackish head. **Where found:** large lakes at most elevations; throughout the Canadian Rockies; small populations in northern Montana and Idaho.

Eared Grebe
Podiceps nigricollis
LENGTH: 12–14 in (30–36 cm)

Long, flattened, 'lobate' toes on legs placed toward the back of the body help propel this small grebe underwater as it hunts for aquatic insects, fish, and crustaceans. Nesting in single pairs or in large colonies, both sexes build 1 or more floating nests of vegetation. Look for the fan-shaped ear tufts and the all-black neck to distinguish it from the horned grebe (*P. auritus*) found in the northern Rockies. **Where found:** lakes, ponds, and marshes; throughout the Rockies, except northern B.C.

Western Grebe
Aechmophorus occidentalis
LENGTH: 20–25 ¼ in (51–64 cm)

The elegant, synchronous courtship dance of a pair of western grebes is one of nature's most beautiful and romantic spectacles. Gregarious by nature, these large grebes often nest in large colonies. Their proficient diving skills and long, sharp bills allow them to spear fish and catch a variety of aquatic invertebrates. Watch for the downy, whitish-gray young riding on the backs of their parents. **Where found:** lakes, ponds, and marshes with shoreline cattails, rushes, and sedges; breeding colonies throughout most of the U.S. Rockies.

Great Blue Heron
Ardea herodias
LENGTH: 50–54 in (127–137 cm)

Numerous large, bulging stick platforms—built high in the towering trees overlooking a mountain wetland—represent the colonial nests, or 'rookery,' of great blue herons. It takes patience to watch, and not disturb, a hunting heron standing motionless in shallow water, waiting to spear anything that swims by. Fish, birds, frogs, snakes, turtles, salamanders, insects, and small mammals are all fair game for the deadly accurate heron, which regurgitates meals for its young. **Where found:** marshes and the edges of lakes, ponds, and rivers; throughout the U.S. and southern Canadian Rockies.

Sandhill Crane
Grus canadensis
LENGTH: 40–50 in (102–127 cm)

This tall, stately bird is a joy to behold. During spring migration and early summer, you might behold the raucous flapping and leaping of a pair of cranes engaged in their courtship dance. A pair of cranes may mate for life, which can mean more than 30 years in the wild. With omnivorous diets, they forage by slowly walking on land or through shallow water. Their grayish body is occasionally tinged with a rusty-red color. **Where found:** marshes, bogs, and open grasslands or meadows surrounded by forest; northern Canadian Rockies, southwestern Montana, southeastern Idaho, western Wyoming, northern Utah, and northern Colorado.

Sora
Porzana carolina
LENGTH: 8–10 in (20–25 cm)

Two ascending whistles, followed by a descending, 'whinnying' call, announce the presence of the near-invisible sora. A member of the Rail Family, its laterally compressed body and long toes allow it to weave through dense jungles of cattails, sedges, and rushes without attracting the attention of potential predators. It feeds on seeds, insects, and mollusks, and nests in a cup of vegetation woven among the cattails. If you are lucky, you might happen upon a sora on one of those rare occasions when it emerges from its tangled marshy home. **Where found:** marshes and wet meadows; throughout the Rockies.

American Coot
Fulica americana
LENGTH: 13–16 in (33–41 cm)

Generalists in both their food and habitat preferences, these commonly seen marshland birds have adapted well to human settled environments that have provided for wetland habitat. They forage by gleaning from the water surface, tipping and diving, or even grazing on land to satisfy their omnivorous diets. Adults aggressively defend the area around their floating nest of dead marshy vegetation by charging at intruders, often running along the water surface. Both adults incubate their eggs and help to raise their precocial young. **Where found:** lakes, ponds, and marshes; throughout the Rockies.

Trumpeter Swan
Cygnus buccinator
LENGTH: 60–72 in (1.5–1.8 m)

This magnificent and powerful bird is the largest native North American waterfowl. The Rocky Mountain population, which by 1912 was nearly extinct owing to hunting and habitat destruction, is currently thriving and expanding. This swan uses its long neck to probe the bottom of ponds and lakeshores for plants and mollusks. Nesting swans will drive away other swans or geese within sight, but they are extremely sensitive to disturbance by humans. **Where found:** lakes, ponds, and large rivers in and around Yellowstone National Park support year-round and overwintering populations; also breeds along the foothills and eastern slopes of west-central Alberta.

Canada Goose
Branta canadensis
LENGTH: 22–48 in (55–122 cm)

At dusk, Canada geese fly in V-formation back to water after a day of foraging abroad. The echo of their honking is a prevalent Rocky Mountain sound. A pair of Canada geese will remain together for life, each year raising, teaching, and aggressively defending 2–11 young. Traditionally migrating north in spring and south in fall, these geese have adapted well to human urbanization and now often remain in urban areas year-round. **Where found:** lakes, ponds, rivers, fields, and parks; throughout the Rockies.

Mallard
Anas platyrhynchos
LENGTH: 20–28 in (51–71 cm) long

The ubiquitous mallard is probably the most recognized duck in all of North America. Mallards are described as puddle or dabbling ducks because of their feeding behavior and choice of habitat. Feeding takes place in shallow water, and involves dunking their heads below the surface in search of aquatic vegetation and associated aquatic invertebrates, leaving us with a view of their tipped-up tails. A good field mark is the purplish-blue speculum bordered by white. **Where found:** lakes, ponds, marshes, and parks; abundant throughout the Rockies.

Northern Pintail

Anas acuta

LENGTH: Male: 25¼–30 in (64–76 cm)
Female: 20–22 in (51–56 cm)

Admired by many people for its long, elegant lines and graceful manner, the northern pintail is often seen foraging in shallow ponds and marshes. Like other puddle ducks, it is able to launch itself into flight from a stationary floating position, rather than having to run along the water surface for long distances as the diving ducks do. This ability allows puddle ducks to escape dangerous, silent predators, including the red fox and bobcat. **Where found:** ponds and marshes; throughout the Rockies.

Blue-winged Teal

Anas discors

LENGTH: 14–16 in (36–41 cm)

An attractive member of Rocky Mountain marsh communities, the blue-winged teal has a taste for the seeds of grasses, sedges, and aquatic plants. Although it will 'tip' its head under water like other dabbling ducks, it prefers to glean seeds, vegetation, and invertebrates from the water surface. Courtship displays and mating occur on the water, but nesting females fly or waddle to grassy meadows or shrubby areas to build a nest, often hundreds of yards away from water. **Where found:** shallow ponds, sloughs, and marshes; throughout the Rockies.

Harlequin Duck
Histrionicus histrionicus
LENGTH: 14–19 in (36–48 cm)

The striking, bold markings of this bird match its daring, fast-water swimming talents. After resting on slippery mid-stream rocks to rest, this duck dives into the cold mountain water, swimming against the current in search of aquatic insect larvae. You might even see it standing on the bottom of the stream, prying up insects from under rocks and gravel. **Where found:** fast-flowing mountain rivers and streams; from B.C. and Alberta to western Wyoming.

Barrow's Goldeneye
Bucephala islandica
LENGTH: 16–20 in (41–51 cm)

The crescent-shaped facial patch of the male Barrow's goldeneye distinguishes it from the similar common goldeneye (*B. clangula*), which has a round facial patch. This diving duck feeds on mollusks, crustaceans, and aquatic invertebrates, and nests in tree cavities or rock crevices. Although most winter along the Pacific coast, some winter from Montana and Idaho, south to Colorado, in mountain ponds warmed by hot springs. **Where found:** lakes, ponds, and rivers at most elevations; B.C., Alberta, Idaho, western Montana, and northwestern Wyoming.

Ruddy Duck
Oxyura jamaicensis
LENGTH: 15–16 in (38–41 cm)

Their unusual color combination, cocked tails, and comical courtship displays have earned male ruddy ducks the reputation of being the clowns of the marsh. But it's the females who play the practical jokes: they often lay their eggs in the nests of other female ruddy ducks or even in the nests of canvasback (*Aythya valisineria*) and redhead (*A. americana*) ducks. This behavior, called 'brood parasitism,' often works because most female birds will incubate the intruder's eggs along with their own! **Where found:** lakes, ponds, and marshes; throughout the Rockies.

Hooded Merganser
Lophodytes cucullatus
LENGTH: 16–19 in (41–48 cm)

Like the common merganser, the smaller hooded merganser is a diving bird that feeds primarily on fish and aquatic invertebrates, nesting in the cavities of mature shoreline trees. The adult male is particularly attractive, using its raised head-crest and dashing winter courtship displays to impress females. Pair bonds are usually formed on their freshwater wintering grounds along the Pacific coast, before spring migration. **Where found:** wooded lakes, marshes, and rivers; B.C., Alberta, northern Idaho, and northern Montana.

Common Merganser
Mergus merganser
LENGTH: 22–27 in (56–69 cm)

These diving birds are similar in shape to the common loon (p. 59). They are equipped with serrated bills to help them grasp and hold the fish, mollusks, and crustaceans that form the basis of their diet. However, unlike loons and grebes, female mergansers lay their 8–11 buff-colored eggs in a tree cavity lined with vegetation. **Where found:** wooded lakes and rivers; throughout the Rockies in summer; usually year-round in the U.S. Rockies.

Turkey Vulture
Cathartes aura
LENGTH: 26–32 in (66–81 cm)

Soaring high above the ground on thermal air currents, the scavenging turkey vulture scours the earth below for signs of its next carrion meal. It is identified in flight by its massive two-toned wings spanning up to 6 ft (2 m), usually held in a V-shaped angle. The vulture's powerful sense of smell is rare among birds: it is able to detect the smell of rotting flesh from over 10 mi (16 km) away. **Where found:** open forests, shrublands, grasslands, and farmlands; from Montana and Idaho south.

Bald Eagle
Haliaeetus leucocephalus
LENGTH: 30–43 in (76–109 cm)

Although most bald eagles breed in Canada and Alaska, some local populations continue to breed in the wilds of the U.S. Rockies. These skilled, opportunistic feeders are known to scavenge extensively, as well as hunt. Fish constitute the bulk of their diet in most habitats throughout much of the year. The banning of DDT and other lethal pesticides has resulted in a glorious comeback for this much-admired bird of prey. **Where found:** breeds close to lakes, large beaver ponds, rivers, and reservoirs; often seen in fields and open country through winter and during migration.

Golden Eagle
Aquila chrysaetos
LENGTH: 30–40 in (76–102 cm)

Magnificent, graceful, and powerful are words that describe the revered golden eagle. The Rocky Mountains provide a perfect home for this impressive hunter. Steep rocky cliffs supply secure nesting sites, and wild mountain peaks, slopes, and valleys produce a wide diversity of prey. Fortuitous observers may watch a breeding pair hunting together to increase their killing efficiency or share in their breathtaking aerial acrobatics. These eagles have long, broad wings with a span often exceeding 6½ ft (2 m). **Where found:** most open habitats at most elevations; throughout the Rockies.

Osprey
Pandion haliaetus
LENGTH: 22–25 in (56–64 cm)

Locked in a perilous head-first dive, an osprey thrusts
its feet through the water's surface. As the silvery spray
subsides, it emerges with a shining rainbow trout in its
clutches. With the fish's head facing forward, the osprey
returns to its ramshackle nest to feed its ravenous young.
Just another great day of fishing for the amazing 'fish-hawk!' In
flight osprey wings often form a prominent M-shape. **Where found:**
lakes and large rivers; throughout most of the Rockies; absent in parts of
Colorado and New Mexico.

Northern Goshawk
Accipiter gentilis
LENGTH: 21–23 in (53–58 cm)

The northern goshawk is an agile and powerful forest
predator able to negotiate lightning-fast turns and crash
through dense forest cover to overtake its nimble prey.
Goshawks have even been known to run on the ground
through thick underbrush to finish off elusive birds or
small mammals. Equally ferocious is their aggressive nest
defense behavior. Those who wander too close to a goshawk
nest are occasionally assaulted in an almost deafening, squawking dive-bomb
attack, involving razor-sharp talons scraped across the highest body part!
Where found: coniferous and mixed forests; throughout the Rockies.

Red-tailed Hawk
Buteo jamaicensis
LENGTH: Male: 18–22³⁄₄ in (46–58 cm)
Female: 20–25¹⁄₄ in (51–64 cm)

This most familiar hawk of the Rockies is easily identified by its rusty-red tail; however, many of the darker
phase or immature individuals lack this distinctive
feature. A member of the Buteos, or soaring hawks,
the red-tailed hawk can frequently be seen flying
high in the sky, searching for unwary ground squirrels, voles, and other small
animals. But its main hunting technique is to perch in a tree, or on a fencepost or
telephone pole, and wait for something to move. Look for the distinct dark band
across the abdomen. **Where found:** in most open-edged habitats; throughout the
Rockies.

American Kestrel
Falco sparverius
Length: 7½–10¼ in (19–26 cm)

If you are watching a small, colorful, sharp-winged bird hovering low above a roadside meadow, then you are seeing the smallest falcon of the Rockies—the American kestrel. This beautiful bird has a diverse carnivorous diet, but relies heavily upon large terrestrial insects. Its diminutive size allows it to nest in the shelter of tree cavities, where both parents help to raise 4–6 young. **Where found:** most open habitats, including roadsides, farmyards, and forest edges; throughout the Rockies.

Peregrine Falcon
Falco peregrinus
Length: Male: 15–17 in (38–43 cm)
Female: 17–19 in (43–48 cm)

Still considered endangered throughout much of its original range after pesticides used in the 1940s–70s decimated its populations, the peregrine is making a strong recovery in the Rockies. Hunting falcons fly at high altitudes, swooping down on flying birds at speeds of 150 mph (240 km/h) or more, instantly killing or knocking its prey to the ground with its clenched feet. **Where found:** open habitats in close proximity to cliffs, which may include city skyscrapers; throughout the Rockies.

Great Horned Owl
Bubo virginianus
Length: 18–25 in (46–64 cm)

The familiar *hoo-hoo-hoooo hoo-hoo* resounding throughout campgrounds and farmyards is the call of this adaptable and superbly camouflaged owl. It is a powerful hunter willing to attack and eat any small creature that moves, including rabbits, pocket gophers, muskrats, voles, snakes, hawks, songbirds, and even skunks. Many owls prey only on food that can be swallowed whole, but the great horned owl uses its strong talons and sharp beak to tear apart larger meals. **Where found:** most open habitats and forest edges; throughout the Rockies.

Great Gray Owl
Strix nebulosa

LENGTH: 24–33 in (61–84 cm)

Large concave facial disks collect the slightest of sounds into asymmetrically placed ear openings (1 ear higher than the other), allowing the great gray owl to triangulate the precise location of a vole munching on seeds under 2 ft (60 cm) of snow. The owl descends from its perch, and hovers briefly before plunging feet first into the snow. With a little squeeze of the talons and a few freeing twists, the owl returns to its perch to swallow its meal whole. **Where found:** coniferous and mixed forests; from B.C. and Alberta to northwestern Wyoming.

Blue Grouse
Dendragapus obscurus

LENGTH: Male: 17–19 in (43–48 cm)
Female: 18–22 in (46–56 cm)

The low, penetrating hoots of the displaying male blue grouse are amplified by its red to yellow, inflated air sacs. Although all birds use air sacs like mammals use lungs, the male blue grouse is able to expose his in attempts to woo potential mates. This grouse is remarkably tolerant of humans, often allowing people to approach within arm's-reach. **Where found:** forest edges and open woodlands at most elevations in summer; dense coniferous forests at higher elevations in winter; throughout the Rockies.

White-tailed Ptarmigan
Lagopus leucurus

LENGTH: 12–14 in (31–36 cm)

White-tailed ptarmigans molt 3 times each year to ensure their plumage blends perfectly with their surrounding environment. In winter they become all white with a thin, red eye comb. They subsist year-round by eating the twigs, leaves, buds, flowers, and seeds of stunted alpine shrubs and forbs. They survive the harsh winds, icy snow, and freezing temperatures of high elevations by excavating snow burrows. These subnivean shelters maintain temperatures close to the freezing mark, allowing ptarmigans to weather the most brutal of winter storms. **Where found:** year-round resident of alpine tundra; throughout the Canadian Rockies and in disjunct, localized populations throughout the U.S. Rockies.

Killdeer
Charadrius vociferus
LENGTH: 9–11 in (23–28 cm)

Ubiquitous and demanding your immediate attention throughout each summer, the vociferous killdeer is an easily identified member of the Plover Family. It is famous for its self-proclaiming call and outstanding performance of the 'broken-wing act,' which is used to draw potential predators away from its egg-filled nest. Four cryptically camouflaged eggs are laid in a shallow scrape in soil or gravel, occasionally lined with pebbles, vegetation, or other debris to improve the disguise. Notice the orangy-brown rump patch when in flight or during the broken wing act. **Where found:** fields, meadows, riparian areas, mudflats, beeches, and shorelines; throughout the Rockies.

Spotted Sandpiper
Actitis macularia
LENGTH: 7–8 in (18–20 cm)

Watch for the distinctive repeated tail bobbing of this dainty, flighty shorebird as it dashes along the shoreline in search of invertebrates. Unlike most smaller birds, the female is larger than the male, and will mate with up to 5 males in a single breeding season. After each mating, the female lays 4 or so eggs and then disappears, leaving the male to incubate the eggs and raise the young alone. **Where found:** shorelines of lakes, ponds, rivers, and streams; throughout the Rockies.

California Gull
Larus californicus
LENGTH: 18–21 in (46–53 cm)

Often thought of as bothersome 'garbage birds,' gulls are truly beautiful and highly adaptable birds. Although they will eat just about anything, breeding California gulls feed largely on invertebrates gleaned from the surface of water or land. They are colony nesters and high flyers. Each fall they migrate to the Pacific coast where they forage for fish or scavenge for the occasional fast-food scrap. **Where found:** lakes, marshes, irrigated fields, and urban areas; Montana and southern Idaho; may also be seen in Wyoming, Utah, and Colorado.

Forster's Tern
Sterna forsteri
LENGTH: 14–16 in (36–41 cm)

More common in the Rockies than the similar looking
common tern (*S. hirundo*), the Forster's tern is a skilled
flyer and precision hunter. Watch for terns hovering
over the water surface in search of fish. Once it locates a fish, it quickly folds its
wings and dives to take its prey just below the surface. People and animals ven-
turing too close to a colony of nesting terns may find themselves being subjected
to a dive-bombing aerial attack from angry, screaming adult terns. **Where found:**
lakes and marshes; Idaho, western Montana, and Colorado.

Rock Dove
Columba livia
LENGTH: 12–13 in (31–33 cm)

The adaptable rock dove is familiar to most
urban and rural dwellers as the common city-
dwelling pigeon. Native to Eurasia, it was
domesticated by humans for a variety of purposes, and
has since been introduced around the world. The high, steep
cliffs of the Rocky Mountains have helped populations of this bird return to their
ancestral, wild ways. Plumage varies from pure white to gray to all black, but is
traditionally gray with an iridescent head. **Where found:** steep cliffs, bridges,
farmyards, parks, and urban areas; throughout the U.S. and southern Canadian
Rockies. **Also known as:** pigeon.

Mourning Dove
Zenaida macroura
LENGTH: 11–13 in (28–33 cm)

The mournful, cooing call of the mourning
dove is often mistaken for the call of an owl.
This bird is always abundant in open
farmyards and along roadsides at lower
elevations, and is commonly seen sitting on
fenceposts and telephone wires. Nestling
doves are fed a protein-rich liquid known as
'pigeon's milk' that is secreted and regurgitated from the crop of both
adults. Adult mourning doves feed almost exclusively on seeds. Sandy grit is
swallowed regularly to aid digestion. **Where found:** any open to semi-open
habitats; throughout the Rockies.

Red-naped Sapsucker
Sphyrapicus nuchalis
LENGTH: 8¼–8¾ in (21–22 cm)

Like the closely related yellow-bellied sapsucker (*S. varius*) of the north and east, this bird is known for the series of shallow parallel holes or 'sap wells' it drills into the bark of living trees and shrubs. When foraging, it flies from tree to tree, drinking the oozing sap and eating insects caught in the sticky juice. These wells rarely harm the trees and may even attract a variety of humming-birds and songbirds. **Where found:** forests, wooded riparian areas, and orchards; throughout the U.S. Rockies and all but the most northern Canadian Rockies.

Downy Woodpecker
Picoides pubescens
LENGTH: 6–7 in (15–18 cm)

Smallest of the Rocky Mountain woodpeckers, the downy is commonly seen in forests, riparian areas, orchards, parks, and backyards with trees. Its markings are virtually identical to the hairy wood-pecker (*P. villosus*), which is considerably larger, has a bill as long as its head, and lacks the black spots on its outer tail feathers. Both woodpeckers fly from tree to tree, foraging for insects on or under-neath the bark. **Where found:** in a wide variety of habitats; throughout the Rockies.

Three-toed Woodpecker
Picoides tridactylus
LENGTH: 8¼–9½ in (21–24 cm)

The three-toed woodpecker lives in dense forests dominated by spruce, fir, and pine, where it finds shelter, nesting sites, and plenty of tree-inhabiting insects. It can be particularly abun-dant in areas infested with wood-boring beetle larvae, espe-cially burned-over areas with lots of standing dead trees. It forages by flaking off large patches of bark from dead or dying trees. The accumulation of dislodged bark chunks at tree bases is a valuable sign of this woodpecker's presence. Only the males have a yellow cap. **Where found:** coniferous forests; throughout the Rockies.

Northern Flicker

Colaptes auratus

LENGTH: 13 in (33 cm)

Flashing red or yellow wings and tail announce your meeting with the northern flicker. This colorful woodpecker is 1 of 2 races; the yellow-shafted flicker of the northern and eastern Rockies and the red-shafted variety of the west. The underside of the wings and tail are accordingly red or yellow. Interbreeding populations along the eastern slopes of the Rockies may have orangy tail and wing feather shafts. The head markings vary between races and gender. **Where found:** most treed habitats, preferring semi-open areas; throughout the Rockies.

Pileated Woodpecker

Dryocopus pileatus

LENGTH: 16–19 in (41–48 cm)

Huge, crow-sized proportions require this woodpecker to eat large amounts of its favorite food—carpenter ants. Large rectangular holes excavated in dead trees are evidence of the pileated woodpecker's zealous hammerings. Although you would think this woodpecker's constant drilling would knock itself senseless, its bony, reinforced skull and cushioned inner casing effectively protect the bird's brain from repeated shock. This species' survival depends on the availability of large, standing, dead trees, naturally found in old-growth forests. **Where found:** coniferous and mixed forests; from B.C. and Alberta to northern Montana and Idaho.

Common Nighthawk
Chordeiles minor
LENGTH: 8¾–10¼ in (22–26 cm)

Members of the cryptic Nightjar Family, common nighthawks can often be heard and seen flying erratically in the summer sky at dusk. They use their unusually wide, gaping mouths to scoop up flying insects in their mid-air swarms. During the day they tend to sleep while perched on a large tree limb. Females typically lay and incubate 2 eggs on a bare patch of ground, without building a nest. Nighthawks winter in South America. **Where found:** mountain slopes and open pine forests; throughout the Rockies.

Belted Kingfisher
Ceryle alcyon
LENGTH: 11–14 in (28–36 cm)

Like other kingfishers around the world, this bird specializes in diving for fish. Watch for it sitting on an exposed branch above water, periodically issuing its boisterous, cackling call. When a fish is located, the kingfisher plunges head-first, with wings folded, into the water to snatch its prey with its long, sharp bill. Air-filled bones quickly force the submerged bird back to the surface. It nests in a chamber at the end of a long tunnel dug into a soil bank. **Where found:** lakes, ponds, and rivers; throughout the Rockies.

Calliope Hummingbird
Stellula calliope
LENGTH: 3 in (8 cm)

The smallest bird in North America, flying calliopes look like large flying insects. Tiny females wrap their lichen-covered nests with the silky strands of spider webs, allowing the nest to expand with rapidly growing young. Calliopes eat about half their weight in nectar and insects each day to maintain their high metabolism and heart rate of roughly 1200 beats per minute! **Where found:** mountain meadows, riparian areas, and open forests; from B.C. and Alberta to northwestern Wyoming and northern Utah; seen throughout the Rockies during spring and late summer migrations.

Broad-tailed Hummingbird
Selasphorus platycercus
LENGTH: 4 in (10 cm)

A high-pitched buzz advertises the approach of the flying male broad-tailed hummingbird. This sound is created by air flowing through its primary flight feathers, and apparently aids the tiny bird in defending its feeding territory from other hummingbirds. Lacking pigment in its feathers, this dazzling, acrobatic gem receives its bright colors from light refracting off microscopic air bubbles trapped within its feathers. The female is less vibrant than the male, with buffy-rufous flanks, speckled throat, and rufous-red on the outer tail feathers. **Where found:** mountain meadows and open forests; from southwestern Montana south; populations may exist in western Montana and northern Idaho.

Rufous Hummingbird
Selasphorus rufus
LENGTH: 3½ in (9 cm)

Glittering, coppery mountain sprites, male rufous hummingbirds are bold and aggressive aerial gymnasts, known to chase other hummers and even larger birds away from nectar-rich mountain meadows. Hummingbirds have co-adapted with many tubular wildflowers, such as fireweed, yellow columbine, and bracted honeysuckle. In return for assistance in cross-pollination, hummingbirds receive an energy-rich burst of liquid manna. The female is distinguished from other species by the red on all her tail feathers. **Where found:** mountain meadows, forests, riparian areas, parks, and gardens; from B.C. and Alberta to northwestern Wyoming; seen throughout the Rockies during mid-summer southern migration.

Olive-sided Flycatcher
Contopus cooperi
LENGTH: 7 1/2 in (19 cm)

An early-morning hike through the lush green conifers of the Rockies in early summer reveals a most curious and incessant wild call: *Quick-three-beers! Quick-three-beers!* This human interpretation of the male olive-sided flycatcher's song may be silly, but it is surprisingly accurate. Built with a wide, flattened bill and sensitive hairs at the corners of its beak, called 'vibrissae,' this well-named bird specializes in launching from its perch to snatch flying insects in mid-air—a popular foraging behavior known as 'hawking' or 'flycatching.' **Where found:** coniferous forests and bogs; throughout the Rockies.

Eastern Kingbird
Tyrannus tyrannus
LENGTH: 8 3/4–9 in (22–23 cm)

The prominent and boisterous eastern kingbirds can often be seen sitting on fence-lines and telephone wires at the side of mountain valley roads, and fluttering around urban backyards, parks, and farms. During May and June, males may be observed performing outrageous aerial acrobatics in their attempt to impress eligible females. Both adults assist in raising 3 or 4 young, feeding them berries and juicy insects caught on the wing. Caution is advised when approaching too close to a kingbird nest, because you may find yourself caught in a noisy, swooping attack. **Where found:** open habitats with some trees; throughout the Rockies.

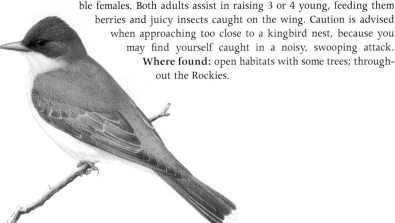

White-throated Swift
Aeronautes saxatalis
LENGTH: 6¾ in (17 cm)

These well-named birds are incredibly fast, often flying up to 100 mph (177 km/h). Their great speed allows them to forage on flying insects far from their nesting sites. They use their saliva to glue nesting materials together into a shallow platform built into a narrow, vertical rock crevice along a steep cliff face. They migrate south for the winter, but usually return to the same nest site. **Where found:** canyons and tall cliffs; throughout the U.S. Rockies but absent from the Canadian Rockies and northern Idaho.

Violet-green Swallow
Tachycineta thalassina
LENGTH: 5 in (13 cm)

The violet-green swallow gracefully glides over mountain treetops and meadows while scooping up tasty flying insects. Similar in appearance to the tree swallow (*T. bicolor*) commonly seen using mountain bluebird boxes, the violet-green is a gentle and curious flyer, often approaching close to observers while engaged in acrobatic foraging feats. This swallow will nest in small colonies or in pairs using tree cavities, as well as nest boxes or crevices and holes in mountain cliffs. **Where found:** open mountain forests and townsites; throughout the Rockies.

Barn Swallow
Hirundo rustica
LENGTH: 7 in (18 cm)

Among the 6 or 7 species of swallows that call the Rocky Mountains their home, the barn swallow is the easiest to recognize; its long, forked tail and rusty-orange throat make it unmistakable. It is commonly seen sitting on telephone wires and fences, or flying about, catching insects in mid-air. The barn swallow has expanded its range across the continent with the aid of humans, who have opened up foraging habitat in previously impenetrable forests and whose buildings provide foundations for swallow nests. **Where found:** open areas near buildings, bridges, or culverts, usually near water; throughout the Rockies.

Gray Jay
Perisoreus canadensis
LENGTH: 11½–12 in (29–30 cm)

These curious, fearless birds won't hesitate to follow you in their search for tasty morsels. Often becoming unusually bold in campgrounds and parking lots, these crafty creatures may steal your lunch right from under your nose! They are known to hide bits of food under the bark of trees, to be retrieved in times of need. Unlike most mountain birds, gray jays build their nests and raise their young in late winter or early spring. Southern birds may have a whitish cap and a gray nape. **Where found:** coniferous forests; throughout the Rockies. **Also known as:** Canada jay, whiskey jack.

Steller's Jay
Cyanocitta stelleri
LENGTH: 11½–12 in (29–30 cm)

Generally shy within the confines of dense, secluded coniferous forests, Steller's jays become jarringly loud and unrelenting thieves in park campgrounds and townsites. Members of the intelligent Corvid Family, these birds are skilled at exploiting edible remnants left by limited human appetites. Devoted parents, these birds remain with their young well into winter to teach them the secrets of foraging and surviving in Rocky Mountain forests. When they are not nesting, Steller's jays prefer to travel in small cohesive flocks. **Where found:** coniferous forests at most elevations; throughout the Rockies.

Western Scrub-Jay
Aphelocoma californica
LENGTH: 12 in (30 cm)

When living at the mercy of unpredictable mountain weather, it's advantageous to be omnivorous like western scrub-jays. Often foraging in pairs or small family groups, on the ground and in trees, they readily accept most seasonally available foods, including seeds, fruit, insects, and the eggs or young of other birds. And when all else fails, these jays may even ride the backs of mule deer and elk to feed on ticks and other ectoparasites! **Where found:** shrublands, canyons, orchards, brushy foothills, and other open habitats; from southern Idaho and southwestern Wyoming south. **Also known as:** Woodhouse's scrub-jay.

Clark's Nutcracker
Nucifraga columbiana
LENGTH: 12–13 in (30–33 cm)

The Clark's nutcracker prefers remote subalpine coniferous forests with an abundance of animal and plant foods. It specializes in harvesting and eating pine seeds, which it caches on south-facing slopes during late summer and fall. A total cache of 30,000 or more seeds helps to sustain a breeding pair throughout winter, and may be used to feed 2–4 young in spring. Both adults help build the nest, incubate the eggs, and feed the young. **Where found:** coniferous forests; throughout the Rockies.

Black-billed Magpie
Pica pica
LENGTH: 18–22 in (46–56 cm)

This bold black and white bird is moderately attractive as it waddles along the ground, foraging to satisfy its omnivorous diet. But when it takes flight, it unfolds a rainbow of shimmering iridescent colors as its wings and glorious long tail flash in the sunlight. Unfortunately, many people find this bird to be as aurally annoying as it is stunningly beautiful! It builds a large, wreath-shaped nest from twigs and branches, and is famous for gathering into large mobs to tease and annoy other birds, such as the great horned owl. **Where found:** most open to semi-open habitats; throughout the Rockies.

Common Raven
Corvus corax
LENGTH: 24 in (61 cm)

The common raven is truly an intelligent, magical being. It possesses a diverse repertoire of calls, maintains a loyal, lifelong pair bond, and has an affinity for outrageous bouts of aerial and terrestrial play. It survives on coastlines, in deserts, on mountains, and in the bitter cold and darkness of the arctic tundra. It also displays the capacity to learn and solve complex problems. **Where found:** in most habitats and at most elevations; throughout the Rockies.

Black-capped Chickadee
Poecile atricapillus
LENGTH: 5–6 in (13–15 cm)

Black-capped chickadees are some of the most common and approachable songbirds in the Rockies. Their cheerful calls and sunny, curious dispositions make them welcome visitors on morning walks and at backyard feeders. They are omnivorous cavity nesters that usually lay 6-8 eggs in late winter or early spring. Small flocks of foraging birds can often be seen swinging upside-down on tree branches, snatching up insects or berries. On cold winter nights, chickadees may huddle together in the shelter of tree cavities or other suitable hollows. **Where found:** mixed and deciduous forests, parks, and suburban backyards; throughout the Rockies.

Mountain Chickadee
Poecile gambeli
LENGTH: 5–5½ in (13–14 cm)

This year-round resident of high-elevation forests tends to feed in the high canopy of conifers. Harsh winter weather can cause these birds to freeze or starve to death, forcing many birds to seek warmer temperatures and more abundant food at lower elevations. In the lower valleys, mountain chickadees often join flocks of black-capped chickadees, brown-capped boreal chickadees (*P. hudsonicus*), and occasionally red-breasted nuthatches. These flocks provide many more eyes to watch for predators and look for good food sources. **Where found:** coniferous forests; throughout the Rockies.

Red-breasted Nuthatch

Sitta canadensis

LENGTH: about 4½ in (11–11.5 cm)

Unlike its white-breasted relative, the red-breasted nuthatch lives almost exclusively in coniferous forests. It survives on insects at various life stages, spiders, and the seeds from conifer cones. It may remain in or near its breeding territory year-round, or may migrate over large distances to find areas with good cone crops. This unusually friendly bird often approaches close to humans, and regularly visits seed and suet feeders during winter. It easily moves headfirst down tree trunks, and may be seen eating carrion to survive frigid mountain winters. **Where found:** coniferous forests; throughout the Rockies.

White-breasted Nuthatch

Sitta carolinensis

LENGTH: 6 in (15 cm)

This bird is commonly seen and heard year-round in riparian areas, along forest edges, in parks, and throughout urban areas with many large deciduous trees. In summer, it specializes in finding and eating insects and spiders. Its ability to walk headfirst down the trunks of trees gives it a unique perspective, allowing it to find insect eggs and pupae that most birds neglect or miss. During winter visits to bird feeders, this bird can be seen flying off to hide the seeds in crevices under the bark of trees. **Where found:** deciduous and mixed forests; southern Canadian Rockies and throughout the U.S. Rockies.

Brown Creeper

Certhia americana

LENGTH: 5 in (13 cm)

The cryptic brown creeper is a rare sight. It feeds on insect eggs, larvae, and adults found hiding in the crevices of tree bark. It forages by creeping up a tree trunk in spirals, then flying to the base of the next tree to continue the process. If startled, it will stop moving and flatten itself against the trunk, making itself virtually invisible against the bark. It nests in old-growth forests with large trees, and is best located by its high-pitched whistling song. **Where found:** coniferous and mixed forests; throughout the Rockies.

Rock Wren
Salpinctes obsoletus
LENGTH: 6 in (15 cm)

Singing male rock wrens bounce their buzzing, trilling songs off the surrounding rocks to maximize the range and aural effect of the sound. Nests are often built in sheltered, rocky crevices, with entrances elaborately 'paved' with small pebbles, bones, and other debris. Its well-camouflaged plumage, secretive habits, and echoing songs and calls can make it difficult to find among the varied, rocky terrain. Its secretive lifestyle leaves much to be learned about this endearing bird. **Where found:** talus slopes, canyons, and rocky areas; throughout the Rockies.

House Wren
Troglodytes aedon
LENGTH: 4¾ in (12 cm)

Boisterous and energetic, the curious house wren is a familiar bird in suburban yards and parks. It is readily identified by its lovely bubbling song and short tail, which is often held straight up. The house wren will apparently nest in any cavity or enclosed space, including woodpecker holes, flowerpots, boots, drain pipes, and even parked cars! Males aggressively defend nesting territories, commonly chasing larger birds and puncturing the eggs of nearby house wrens and other bird species. **Where found:** most lower-elevation habitats; throughout the Rockies.

Ruby-crowned Kinglet

Regulus calendula

LENGTH: 4⅜ in (11 cm)

This spunky bird can easily be confused with a
small flycatcher, owing to its size, 2 white wing bars,
and habit of hawking insects out of mid-air. Its tiny,
black bill, broken eye ring, constant flitting about,
and nervous flicking of its wings, however, betray
its true identity. It prefers foraging and nesting
high above the forest floor in the canopy of spruce, fir,
or pine, migrating to warmer southern climates for winter.
Where found: coniferous forests; throughout the Rockies.

Golden-crowned Kinglet

Regulus satrapa

LENGTH: 4 in (10 cm)

Not much larger than a rufous hummingbird,
the golden-crowned kinglet is difficult to see
as it probes the distant tops of mountain
conifers. It is frequently seen banding together in
roaming multi-species flocks that may include
mountain and boreal chickadees (*Poecile hudsonicus*),
red-breasted nuthatches, three-toed woodpeckers, brown
creepers, and ruby-crowned kinglets. It has an extremely
high-pitched call that is only audible to those with a sensitive sense of hearing.
Where found: coniferous forests; throughout the Rockies.

Blue-gray Gnatcatcher

Polioptila caerulea

LENGTH: 4⅜ in (11 cm)

This long-tailed inhabitant of woodlands and brushy
areas is constantly on the move. With its tail cocked in the air,
it flits from shrub to shrub, gleaning insects from branches and leaf
surfaces. Its small, cup-shaped nest built by both adults is saddled
on the branch of a deciduous tree. Although this bird undoubtedly
eats gnats, these particular insects only represent a tiny part of this bird's
insectivorous diet. The male displays a black eyebrow during breeding season,
and the female is paler in color than the male. **Where found:** open forests and
thickets; from southern Idaho and Wyoming south.

Mountain Bluebird
Sialia currucoides
LENGTH: 7 in (18 cm)

Spectacular in its simplistic brilliance, the mountain bluebird appears as if it were forged from the bluest of Rocky Mountain skies. It can often be seen hovering over open meadows while hunting for insects. Concern over the conservation of this beautiful, cavity-nesting bird resulted in the establishment of bluebird nest box routes. Nest boxes are built, monitored, and maintained with annual cleanings by volunteers throughout much of the Rockies. Volunteering on one of these routes can be a great way of getting close to these fascinating birds. **Where found:** open forests, mountain meadows, and sagebrush; throughout the Rockies.

Townsend's Solitaire
Myadestes townsendi
LENGTH: 8¾ in (22 cm)

A member of the Thrush Family, the Townsend's solitaire is, as its name suggests, solitary in nature. Nests are made on the ground among rocks or at the bases of big spruce or subalpine fir trees where there are natural cavities made by the tree's roots. Insects form the foundation of its summer diet, and the berries of plants such as common juniper and dwarf mistletoe are staples in winter. **Where found:** summers in high-elevation coniferous forests, winters in lower-elevation valleys and open forests; throughout the Rockies.

American Robin
Turdus migratorius
LENGTH: 10 in (25 cm)

It is safe to say that most of us have been introduced to the wonderful American robin. For many of us, its presence on townsite lawns and gardens symbolizes the peaceful co-existence of humans and birds and the arrival of spring. It is commonly seen probing our yards for tantalizing worms and insects to feed its growing young. If you're lucky, a pair may choose to build a nest and raise its spotted young on a tree in your own backyard. **Where found:** most lower-elevation habitats; throughout the Rockies.

Varied Thrush
Ixoreus naevius
LENGTH: 9½ in (24 cm)

Heard far more often than it is seen, the varied thrush conceals its presence within the thick, moist spruce, fir, and hemlock forests of the northern Rockies. Designed to penetrate its dense surroundings to reach the ears of a potential mate, the song of the male varied thrush consists of a number of single note whistles, each spaced a few seconds apart, and delivered at different pitches. **Where found:** dense, moist coniferous forests; B.C., Alberta, northwestern Montana, and northern Idaho.

Plumbeous Vireo
Vireo plumbeus
LENGTH: 5½ in (14 cm)

Like most vireos, plumbeous vireos build hanging nests, which are slung between the forked extensions of horizontal tree branches. These easy-to-find nests are often parasitized by brown-headed cowbirds. Plumbeous vireos forage for insects by carefully investigating tree branches, or by hawking them from the air. Their song sounds like a crude rendition of an American robin's song. Similar in foraging habits and general looks, vireos are distinguished from warblers by their duller colors and thicker bills. Recently the plumbeous vireo has been distinguished from the blue-headed vireo (*V. solitarius*) east of the Continental Divide and Cassin's vireo (*V. cassinii*) west of the Canadian and Northern U.S. Rockies—they were all once called the solitary vireo. **Where found:** coniferous and mixed forests; central and Southern U.S. Rockies.

Western Tanager
Piranga ludoviciana
LENGTH: 7 in (18 cm)

As brightly colored as most tropical birds, attractive western tanagers breed in higher-elevation forests, but may be seen anywhere during spring and fall migration. Their tropical good looks may come from their habit of wintering in the sunny, warm climates of Central and South America, where they feed on juicy insects and sweet tropical fruit. The females have a duller plumage of greenish-yellow with a gray back. **Where found:** coniferous and mixed forests; throughout the Rockies.

Yellow-rumped Warbler

Dendroica coronata

LENGTH: 5½ in (14 cm)

The yellow-rumped warbler is reported to be the most abundant warbler in North America. Unlike most warblers, some yellow-rumps often overwinter in coastal and southern areas of the U.S., allowing them to arrive at preferred spring breeding grounds before most other birds. During the breeding season, adult birds can often be seen carrying insects in their bills as they fly—this observation is usually a sure sign that young are hatched and demanding to be fed. **Where found:** coniferous forests; throughout the Rockies.

Yellow Warbler

Dendroica petechia

LENGTH: 5 in (13 cm)

Often called a wild canary, this beaming yellow warbler seems brighter than the sun. Because it has co-evolved with the brown-headed cowbird on the Great Plains, it is one of the few birds able to recognize and reject cowbird eggs. The yellow warbler is widely abundant, breeding from Mexico to Alaska, and wintering in Central and South America. All birds that breed in North America and winter in the tropics are called neo-tropical migrants. Streaking on the breast of female yellow warblers may be dull but is usually absent. **Where found:** shrubby riparian areas, parks, yards, and gardens; throughout the Rockies.

Townsend's Warbler

Dendroica townsendi

LENGTH: 5 in (13 cm)

The striking contrast of yellow against black sets this warbler on fire! Watching this wood warbler foraging in the high canopy can cause your neck to ache—that is if you can see it. Without the Townsend's warblers' constant flitting and singing, they would remain largely unseen. This bird gleans vegetation and flycatches for beetles, flies, wasps, and caterpillars. **Where found:** old-growth coniferous forests; B.C., Alberta, northwestern Montana, and northern Idaho.

American Redstart

Setophaga ruticilla

LENGTH: 5 in (13 cm)

This magnificent treasure exhibits the hyper-
active feeding habits of its wood warbler kin, often
allowing only fleeting, but dazzling, observations. Its decisive, precision flying makes it an expert at catching insects during quick, flashy
aerial forays. During its low-flying nocturnal migrations, American redstarts and
other birds face numerous dangers. Power lines and towers, telephone poles, and
even skyscrapers become deadly barriers especially during foggy weather. **Where
found:** riparian areas and second-growth woodlands; from B.C. and Alberta to
northern Colorado.

Common Yellowthroat

Geothlypis trichas

LENGTH: 4³/₈–5¹/₂ in (11–14 cm)

Common yellowthroats are busy birds during
nesting season. Females build a nest low to the
ground in small shrubs or among reeds or cattails. They
then lay and incubate 3–5 eggs. Meanwhile, the males are charged with
defending the territory from other males, scolding intruders while leading them
away from the nest, and feeding the female during incubation. Both parents feed the
ever-hungry young and may work overtime if they have unfortunately acquired a
brown-headed cowbird chick—a female cowbird often lays its eggs in yellowthroat
nests. **Where found:** marshes, marshy lakeshores, riparian areas, and wet, shrubby
areas; throughout the Rockies.

Wilson's Warbler

Wilsonia pusilla

LENGTH: 4³/₈–5 in (11–13 cm)

Look for these tiny, spirited warblers
among the tall alders and willows along
mountain streams and beaver ponds. Short
mountain summers mean that a pair of breeding
adults must quickly build their nest and lay their eggs in
anticipation of a brief period of insect hatchings that will feed hungry,
fast-growing young. Wilson's warblers can often be seen hawking insects, or
fluttering up to the undersides of leaves to snatch up hidden insect larvae. **Where
found:** riparian areas and wetlands; throughout the Rockies.

Horned Lark
Eremophila alpestris
LENGTH: 7–7½ in (18–19 cm)

The horned lark is one of the most adaptable and widespread birds in North America, breeding from Mexico to the high arctic islands. It is found at virtually all elevations where there is open ground with low-cropped vegetation. It is most easily seen foraging for seeds and insects on roadsides, often impeding traffic by foraging on gravel roads. Look for the white outer tail feathers on an otherwise long, blackish tail as they flush to safer ground. **Where found:** open fields, croplands, lake shorelines, gravel roads, and alpine tundra; throughout the Rockies.

European Starling
Sturnus vulgaris
LENGTH: 8¼–8¾ in (21–22 cm)

Introduced to New York City in 1890 from Europe, European starlings have been both a success story and a nightmare. Incredibly adaptive, this bird has spread to every treed corner of North America and has thrived in the shadow of human development. However, its success has come at a cost to other species. Being a cavity nester and aggressive in nature, it continues to outcompete many native birds such as mountain bluebirds and tree swallows (*Tachycineta bicolor*) for prime nesting sites and food, resulting in a decline in some native bird populations. **Where found:** urban yards and parks, farmyards, riparian areas, and fields; throughout the Rockies.

Loggerhead Shrike
Lanius ludovicianus
LENGTH: 9 in (23 cm)

Half-songbird, half-raptor, the loggerhead shrike is a formidable winged predator. It feeds primarily on large insects, but is known to take everything from small mammals to small fish. It is also called the 'butcher bird' for its gruesome habit of impaling prey on thorny shrubs or barbed wire fences. Out of the reach of other animals, the food is thus stored for later consumption. Nests, too, are built within the shelter of dense, thorny cover. **Where found:** open to semi-open habitats with trees, shrubs, posts, or high-mounted wires; Montana and southern Idaho south.

Gray Catbird
Dumetella carolinensis
LENGTH: 8¾ in (22 cm)

This member of the Mockingbird Family is equipped
with a loud and highly varied musical repertoire, with
each song often ending in a cat-like *meeeow*. Like other
mockingbirds, a male gray catbird often mimics the calls of other
birds, occasionally inserting parts of these calls into its repertoire.
Most of a catbird's time is spent foraging around dense shrubs and thickets
for insects and berries, or chasing other catbirds during courtship or territorial
defense. **Where found:** tangled thickets, dense shrubby areas, and thick forest
edges; from the extreme southern Canadian Rockies south.

Cedar Waxwing
Bombycilla cedrorum
LENGTH: 7 in (18 cm)

Waxwings are named for the red wax-like droplets on the
tips of their secondary wing feathers. Practiced
observers learn to recognize the presence of these beautiful, polished birds by their high-pitched, trilling calls.
They are highly gregarious birds, often seen feeding in
large flocks on the berries of mountain ash trees. Watch
for courting pairs engaging in their ritualized courtship
displays. Similar-looking Bohemian waxwings *(B. garrulus)* have chestnut undertail coverts, and can be seen throughout the Rockies during some winters. **Where
found:** open forests, orchards, riparian areas, and parks; throughout the Rockies.

American Dipper
Cinclus mexicanus
LENGTH: 7½–8 in (19–20 cm)

Fitted with scaly nose plugs, warm, dense
plumage, and a large oil gland used to waterproof
its feathers, the American dipper spends its entire life
swimming and diving for aquatic insects in frigid Rocky
Mountain streams. It not only 'flies' under the fast-flowing water, but can
also walk on the bottom while searching for tasty insect larvae hiding under rocks
and gravel. In between dives it stands on slippery rocks at the water's edge, bobbing its body up and down. Its mossy, dome-shaped nest is built on rock walls,
exposed tree roots, or behind waterfalls. **Where found:** fast-flowing mountain
streams; throughout the Rockies.

89

Spotted Towhee
Pipilo maculatus
LENGTH: 7–8¾ in (18–22 cm)

The frantic rustle of leaves from deep within a streamside thicket is suddenly accented by 2 curious cat-like calls. After making a few squeaking sounds with your lips, a spotted towhee noisily emerges from its shrubby cover, intent on scolding you for disturbing its breakfast hunt. This bird prefers to forage on the ground by scratching away the forest litter with 2-footed hops. The spotted towhee and the eastern towhee (*P. erythrophthalmus*) were collectively known as the 'rufous-sided towhee' but are now recognized as 2 distinct species. **Where found:** open forests and riparian areas with shrubby understory; from southern Canadian Rockies south.

Chipping Sparrow
Spizella passerina
LENGTH: 5–6 in (13–15 cm)

Named for its long, trilling song, which can be easily confused with that of the dark-eyed junco (p. 91), the chipping sparrow is a pleasant and fairly friendly bird. It is seen in many habitats, including those altered by people. These sparrows typically raise 2 broods of young each summer. Although this practice increases the potential number of young produced each year, it also improves the chances for crafty brown-headed cowbirds to lay eggs in one of their nests. **Where found:** open coniferous forests, riparian areas, forest edges, farms, orchards, and urban parks; throughout the Rockies.

Vesper Sparrow
Pooecetes gramineus
LENGTH: 5½–6¾ in (14–17 cm)

The many species of little brown sparrows found in grassy areas are often distinguished by song because their inconspicuous field marks and tendency to stay hidden makes identification by sight difficult. But the vesper sparrow's unique markings and common use of fenceposts as singing perches should definitely catch your attention. Look for it in grassy areas interspersed with shrubs, under which it usually builds its nest. **Where found:** meadows, fields, roadside fences and ditches, forest clearings, sagebrush, and grassy slopes; throughout the Rockies.

Song Sparrow
Melospiza melodia

LENGTH: 5½–7 in (14–18 cm)

The cheerful, melodious song of the song sparrow, like the songs of other songbirds, serves a number of functions. It identifies the singer as a song sparrow, rather than some other species, it attracts a mate, and it defines the boundaries of a male's breeding territory. By singing from tall shrubs at the edges of its territory, the male song sparrow warns other males to stay off its turf! **Where found:** dense shrubbery bordering open and riparian areas; throughout the Rockies.

White-crowned Sparrow
Zonotrichia leucophrys

LENGTH: 5½–7 in (14–18 cm)

Unmistakable, with its black-and-white–striped crown, this sparrow breeds throughout the Rockies, and often winters in the southern ranges. It usually feeds in flocks of various sizes, and its diet consists of seeds, flowers, buds, berries, and insects. Females build a well-camouflaged, cup-shaped nest on the ground, concealing it from predators such as skunks, foxes, ground squirrels, weasels, and even egg-eating birds and snakes. **Where found:** various habitats, including forest edges, wet meadows, thickets, gardens, parks, and shrubby areas; throughout the Rockies.

Dark-eyed Junco
Junco hyemalis

LENGTH: 5–6¾ in (13–17 cm)

This common bird is regularly seen at the base of trees and shrubs, scratching the ground in its search for seeds and insect larvae. Its familiar single-note calls of *dit*, *tsip*, or *zeet* can be heard year-round, at different elevations depending on the season. This species has been divided into a number of different races. The 'Oregon,' 'Oregon pink-sided,' and 'gray-headed' races may all be found in various parts of the Rockies. The more widely distributed Oregon race has a dark black to gray head and tail, chestnut back, and chestnut or pink sides. **Where found:** coniferous and mixed forests; throughout the Rockies. **Also known as:** Oregon junco.

Yellow-headed Blackbird

Xanthocephalus xanthocephalus

LENGTH: 8–11 in (20–28 cm)

The loud, raw, gronky song of the male yellow-headed blackbird is not like a song at all, but it electrifies the cacophony of Rocky Mountain wetlands. It calls from atop the bulging seed-heads of tall cattails, which act like fenceposts outlining the borders of its breeding territory. When not engaged in courtship or colony nesting, males and females gather in large flocks to feed on seeds and insects found in surrounding fields, pastures, and meadows. **Where found:** marshes and marshy lakeshores; throughout the Rockies.

Red-winged Blackbird

Agelaius phoeniceus

LENGTH: 7½–9½ in (19–24 cm)

The sonorous *Ogalreeee* song, and the flashing red shoulders of the male red-winged blackbird are hallmarks of North American marshes. This common bird is often seen breeding next to colonies of yellow-headed blackbirds. Females build a cup-shaped nest lashed to standing rushes or cattails, so that it hangs above the water or ground surface. Males who fail to display their red shoulder epaulettes are unable to defend a breeding territory and attract a mate. **Where found:** marshes, marshy lakeshores, and wet meadows and ditches; throughout the Rockies.

Western Meadowlark

Sturnella neglecta

LENGTH: 8–9¾ in (20–25 cm)

This bird is a common sight on roadside fenceposts and telephone poles in open grassy habitats, particularly from April to late June when males are issuing their lovely, whistling songs. Nesting on the ground, females build a cup-shaped nest with a grassy dome, making the structure virtually invisible among the surrounding vegetation. Insects, followed by seeds, form the bulk of the melodic meadowlark's diet. **Where found:** fields, pastures, meadows, and grasslands; from extreme southern B.C. and Alberta south.

Brown-headed Cowbird

Molothrus ater

LENGTH: 6–8 in (15–20 cm)

Devious 'brood parasites,' female cowbirds do not build their own nests—instead, they lay their eggs in the nests of other birds. Because most nest owners cannot differentiate the foreign cowbird eggs from their own, they continue to incubate the cowbird eggs, and raise the much larger and aggressive cowbird nestlings—all at the expense of their own young. Regrettably, human activities have allowed cowbirds to expand across the continent, leaving many bird populations in peril. **Where found:** forest edges, fields, pastures, farmyards, riparian areas, and roadsides; throughout the Rockies.

Bullock's Oriole

Icterus bullockii

LENGTH: 7–8¾ in (18–22 cm)

Until recently, this bird was considered to be a western race of the northern oriole. Two distinct species are now recognized as the eastern Baltimore oriole (*I. galbula*) and the western Bullock's oriole. At home primarily in the U.S. Rockies, the Bullock's oriole builds a wonderful hanging nest made from tightly woven plant fibers, grass, and other materials. It is usually located 20–30 ft (6–9 m) above the ground in a tall, shady tree. **Where found:** riparian areas (especially with cottonwoods), forest edges, and tree groves; from extreme southern B.C. and Alberta south.

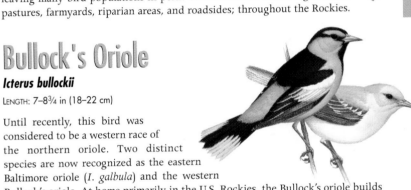

Red Crossbill

Loxia curvirostra

LENGTH: 5½–7 in (14–18 cm)

During your next meeting with these colorful, nomadic birds, use a pair of binoculars to closely examine their unusual bills. Crossed at the tip, the bills are skillfully used to pry open pinecone scales, allowing the tongue to extract the energy-filled seeds locked inside. Their dependence on pinecones forces them to constantly migrate to areas with good cone crops. The male has a red to yellow body, whereas the female is olive-yellow with a gray throat. The similar-looking white-winged crossbill (*L. leucoptera*) has 2 white wing bars, and will feed on spruce and pine. **Where found:** coniferous forests; throughout the Rockies.

Gray-crowned Rosy-Finch
Leucosticte tephrocotis
LENGTH: 5½–6¾ in (14–17 cm)

Ornithologists still debate whether or not this rosy-finch is a distinct species from the black rosy-finch (*L. autrata*) of the central Rockies and the brown-capped rosy-finch (*L. australis*) of the southern Rockies, which all share overlapping ranges. They all specialize in living and breeding in the high alpine, often feeding their young frozen insects and seeds, and roosting in large flocks in caves and mine adits during cold weather. **Where found:** winters in alpine, lower-elevation valleys, and townsites; may winter throughout the Rockies; year-round in Alberta, B.C., Idaho, and Montana.

House Finch
Carpodacus mexicanus
LENGTH: 5–6 in (13–15 cm)

The sweet, warbling song of the house finch is becoming increasingly common throughout the Canadian Rockies as it slowly expands its range to the north, using bird feeders stocked with sunflower seeds to survive cold, snowy mountain winters. These charming, bold birds often allow close observation, but it can be disappointing to watch them selfishly scare away other birds in defense of their 'private' food source. **Where found:** canyons, shrublands, urban parks, and suburban backyards; from southern B.C. and Alberta south.

American Goldfinch
Carduelis tristis
LENGTH: 4⅜–5½ in (11–14 cm)

Commonly seen in roadside thickets and weedy fields, the charming, glowing American goldfinch is always a welcome sight. The female is similar in appearance but has an olive-yellow body. Because it feeds primarily on the late summer seeds of wild plants, this bird is a late nester. Young are fed a partially digested mix of seeds with a few insects, regurgitated from the crops of both parents. Wild sunflower and thistle seeds are this bird's late summer favorites. **Where found:** forest edges and most open habitats interspersed with shrubs and trees; from southern Alberta and B.C. south.

Evening Grosbeak
Coccothraustes vespertinus
LENGTH: 7–8¾ in (18–22 cm)

Thick, crushingly strong but dexterous bills make these birds superbly adapted to eating large seeds. Flashing black-and-white wings and flaring yellowish bodies hint at the approach of a flock of evening grosbeaks foraging for seed-filled shrubs and sunflowers. Nesting females incubate their eggs for 11–14 days. They are often fed by their mates. **Where found:** breeds in coniferous and mixed forests and winters in open forests, shrubby areas, and backyards; throughout the Rockies.

Lazuli Bunting
Passerina amoena
LENGTH: 5½ in (14 cm)

Look for this colorful bunting on shrubby talus slopes bordering a nearby pond or stream. The bright, energetic male is quite conspicuous as it sings from the tops of rocks and shrubs, but the female is often eva-sive, busily foraging or gathering nesting materials. The females have a brownish head and back with a buffy-tan breast, white belly, bluish wings, rump, and tail, and 2 faint wingbars. In southern Colorado and northern New Mexico, the lazuli bunting may interbreed with its pure blue relative, the indigo bunting (*P. cyanea*). **Where found:** open, shrubby areas and shrubby riparian areas; from the central Canadian Rockies south.

House Sparrow
Passer domesticus
LENGTH: 5½–6¾ in (14–17 cm)

Native to Africa and Eurasia, the house sparrow has been introduced around the world, finding suc-cess in its association with human settlement. Many people who enjoy native birds wish that the house sparrow had never been released in New York City in 1851. Its aggressive nature allows it to outcompete and even evict native birds from preferred urban nesting cavities. Much can be learned from this common (year-round), remarkably stubborn, and adaptable bird. **Where found:** farms and urban areas; throughout the Rockies.

AMPHIBIANS & REPTILES

Reptiles and amphibians are commonly referred to as cold-blooded, but this is misleading because reptiles and amphibians often maintain their bodies at a higher temperature than most mammals. These animals are ectothermic: the temperature of the surrounding environment governs their body temperature. The animal will obtain heat from sunlight, warm rocks and logs, and warmed earth. Reptiles and amphibians hibernate in winter in cold regions, and some species of reptiles estivate in summer in hot regions. **Reptiles** are fully terrestrial vertebrates with scaly skin. In this guide the representatives are skinks, turtles, lizards, and snakes. Most reptiles lay eggs buried in loose soil, but some snakes and lizards give birth to live young. Reptiles do not have a larval stage. Snakes will molt as they grow to larger body sizes. **Amphibians** are smooth-skinned and most often live in moist habitats. They are represented by the salamanders, frogs, and toads. They typically lay soft-shelled eggs in jelly-like masses in water. These eggs hatch into gilled larvae (larvae of frogs and toads are called tadpoles), which then metamorphose into adults with lungs and legs. Amphibians can regenerate their skin and often entire limbs. Male and female amphibians often differ in size and color, and males may have other diagnostics when sexually mature, such as vocal sacs in many frogs and toads.

AMPHIBIANS

Tiger Salamander
Ambystoma tigrinum
LENGTH: 5–12 in (13–31 cm)

Tiger salamanders are considered to be the world's largest terrestrial salamanders and can live for up to 16 years. Adults spend most of their time underground and are rarely seen out in the open, except during rainy periods throughout the spring breeding season. They often use animal burrows near water. Their coloration is highly variable: generally yellow, cream, green, gray, or brown, with black spots, blotches, bars, or reticulate patterns. **Where found:** from grasslands and sagebrush to subalpine forests and meadows up to 11,000 ft (3350 m); from extreme southern border of B.C. and Alberta south.

Western Long-toed Salamander

Ambystoma macrodactylum

LENGTH: 3⅛–4¾ in (8–12 cm)

These striking, secretive creatures occasionally hide or feed on invertebrates under rocks or decomposing logs. Active primarily at night, they are more easily seen in the rainy months of April and May when they migrate to their breeding sites in silt-free ponds and lakes. Eggs laid singly or in clumps on rocks or vegetation take about 3 weeks to hatch. Embryonic salamanders obtain their life-sustaining oxygen through the egg's gas-permeable walls. **Where found:** arid, low-elevation sagebrush to subalpine and alpine forests; B.C., Alberta, Montana, and Idaho.

Pacific Giant Salamander

Dicamptodon ensatus

LENGTH: 7–11½ in (18–29 cm)

Unlike most salamanders, which are typically nocturnal, the Pacific giant often crawls about the forest floor during daylight hours. It has been known to climb trees and shrubs up to 8 ft (2.5 m), and may give a low-pitched alarm call when captured. These large salamanders rarely bite people although scars on their tails indicate battles with each other. **Where found:** moist forests along mountain streams and lakes; extreme west-central Montana and northern Idaho.

Van Dyke's Salamander

Plethodon vandykei

LENGTH: 2½–4½ in (6.5–11 cm)

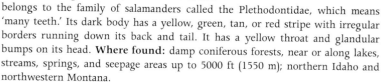

Unlike other salamanders of the Rockies, the Van Dyke's salamander is lungless; instead of breathing with lungs, it breathes through its thin, moist skin. It also belongs to the family of salamanders called the Plethodontidae, which means 'many teeth.' Its dark body has a yellow, green, tan, or red stripe with irregular borders running down its back and tail. It has a yellow throat and glandular bumps on its head. **Where found:** damp coniferous forests, near or along lakes, streams, springs, and seepage areas up to 5000 ft (1550 m); northern Idaho and northwestern Montana.

Tailed Frog
Ascaphus truei
LENGTH: 1–2 in (2.5–5 cm)

This remarkable nocturnal frog usually lives close to cold mountain streams where it lays its eggs from May to September. Eggs are laid on the downstream side of rocks, and take 6 months to hatch. Tadpoles survive in frigid, fast-flowing water by clinging to rocks with their suction cup-like mouths, eating algae and diatoms. Adults are green, gray, brown, or reddish-brown with dark spots or mottling, a pale yellow to green triangle on the snout, a pinkish belly, and a tail-like copulatory organ. **Where found:** cold, fast-flowing mountain streams; western Montana, northern Idaho, and near the extreme southern border of B.C. and Alberta.

Great Basin Spadefoot
Scaphiopus intermontanus
LENGTH: 1½–2½ in (4–6.5 cm)

Spadefoot toads are named for the dark, wedge-shaped 'spade' found near the heel of their hind feet. Like most spadefoot toads, the Great Basin spadefoot burrows underground during the day and hunts for insects at night. This relatively smooth-skinned toad has an olive-green to grayish-green back with many small black and red tubercles and a small hump between its eyes. Its call is a loud *wa-wa-wa*. **Where found:** from low-elevation sagebrush to higher-elevation spruce-fir communities up to 9200 ft (2800 m); Idaho, Wyoming, Utah, and Colorado.

Northern Leopard Frog
Rana pipiens
LENGTH: 2–5 in (5–13 cm)

The northern leopard frog relies on unpolluted aquatic environments its whole life. Eggs are laid on aquatic vegetation, tadpoles feed and grow in water, and metamorphosed adults rely on water to escape from danger. Adults eat insects, spiders, fish, other frogs, and even small snakes. There has been great concern over the drastic declines in northern leopard frog populations during the past few decades. **Where found:** in or near marshes, ponds, streams, springs, and other permanent water sources with sufficient vegetation at various elevations; from Alberta and B.C. south.

Spotted Frog
Rana pretiosa
LENGTH: 2–4 in (5–10 cm)

The spotted frog forages throughout the day for insects and other invertebrates. It tends to be sluggish when approached, but will jump for cover in water and aquatic vegetation when threatened. Its back forms ridges similar to those found on the northern leopard frog. Color is variable with a brown to bronze-colored back, light spots surrounded by black on the back, a red, orange, or yellow belly, and pink or red on the inside of the hind legs. A dark mask around the eyes can be present. **Where found:** in or near high-elevation lakes, ponds, and streams with emergent vegetation; B.C. and Alberta to northwestern Wyoming and northeastern Utah.

Wood Frog
Rana sylvatica
LENGTH: 1¼–3⅛ in (3–8 cm)

The wood frog is a true natural wonder— during winter hibernation its body will actually freeze solid! To survive this condition, it produces a natural antifreeze that keeps the body cells from bursting or dehydrating. In spring, warmer temperatures thaw the frog's icy body, allowing regular body functions to return to normal! **Where found:** from montane grasslands to subalpine forests near ponds, marshes, or other sources of water; common in B.C. and Alberta, and small population pockets in northern Idaho and Montana, Wyoming and Colorado.

Western Toad
Bufo boreas
LENGTH: 2¼–5 in (5.5–13 cm)

Touching a toad will not give you warts, but the western toad does have a way of discouraging our unwanted affections! When handled, it secretes a toxin from large parotid glands behind its eyes, which acts to irritate the mouth of potential predators. This large, gray, green, or brown toad is great at catching insects and other tasty invertebrates, including worms and slugs. **Where found:** moist forests and meadows in the foothills, montane, and subalpine zones; throughout the Rockies. **Also known as:** boreal toad.

Pacific Treefrog
Hyla regilla
LENGTH: ¾–2 in (2–5 cm)

Pacific treefrogs are a joy to watch. Their adhesive toe pads allow them to climb vertical surfaces and cling to the tiniest branch. They can also change color within a few minutes, allowing them to blend into their immediate habitat. Colors include green, brown, gray, tan, reddish, and black; dark spots are often present. **Where found:** lower-elevation shrublands and riparian areas; B.C., Idaho, and northwestern Montana.

Boreal Chorus Frog
Pseudacris triseriata
LENGTH: ¾–1½ in (2–4 cm)

Although they are members of the Treefrog Family, boreal chorus frogs spend most of their time feeding on or near the ground. The warm, rainy nights of March and April are often alive with the choruses of vocal male frogs attempting to attract a mate. Their call sounds like a fingernail running down the teeth of a comb. Their color varies from green to brown or gray. **Where found:** grasslands, shrublands, riparian areas, and forests, usually near water; from lower elevations of the Alberta Rockies to high-elevation mountains of Central and Southern U.S. Rockies. **Also known as:** striped chorus frog.

REPTILES

Western Painted Turtle
Chrysemys picta
LENGTH: 2½–10¼ in (6.5–26 cm)

Painted turtles can often be seen basking in the sun on top of floating logs, mats of vegetation, or exposed rocks. When alarmed, they slip into the water for a quick escape. These turtles may live for up to 40 years. The oval shell of the back, called a 'carapace,' is olive, black, or brown with red, yellow, and/or green underside borders. **Where found:** marshes, ponds, lakes, and slow-flowing streams at lower elevations; primarily in Montana, but also in small areas of B.C., northern Idaho, Wyoming, southwestern Colorado, and northwestern New Mexico.

Eastern Short-horned Lizard
Phrynosoma douglassi
LENGTH: 1½–5 in (4–13 cm)

The cryptic disguise of this lizard makes it almost impossible to spot, and its spiny armor makes it difficult for predators to eat. Its feeding strategy is to sit and wait for ants, beetles, or grasshoppers to pass by. Your best chance at spotting this lizard is to walk through its favorite habitat and watch for any sudden movements. **Where found:** flat, arid habitats with sage and rocks or sand at lower elevations in the north and higher elevations in the south; from southern Idaho and Montana south.

Sagebrush Lizard
Sceloporus graciosus
LENGTH: 1½–5 in (4–13 cm)

Active during the warm daylight hours, these lizards pursue beetles, ants, insects, spiders, mites, and ticks on the ground or in small trees and shrubs. All reptiles regulate their body temperature by moving into suitable ambient environmental conditions. Basking on sun-warmed rocks helps sagebrush lizards warm up. Males have dark blue belly patches and blue mottling on the throat; females have pink to orange sides and neck. **Where found:** rocky areas, stone piles, and sagebrush communities, occasionally in open forested areas at higher elevations; from southern Montana and Idaho south.

Northern Alligator Lizard
Gerrhonotus coeruleus
LENGTH: 6–13 in (15–33 cm)

Look for this secretive lizard sunning itself on top of rocks on summer days. This lizard is the primary host for the young life stages of the tick, *Ixodes pacificus*, commonly found on wild mammals and livestock. This lizard prefers open, rocky areas close to forest cover. It is olive-green, brown, or bluish-gray in color with a conspicuous fold of skin along its sides; young have a brown back, blackish sides, and a light dorsal stripe extending down their backs. **Where found:** beneath rocks, logs, or vegetative litter in moist forests; southern B.C., northern Idaho, and western Montana.

Western Skink
Eumeces skiltonianus
LENGTH: 2½–3¼ in (6.5–8.5 cm)

This reptile is diurnal and secretive, and feeds on invertebrates. It spends much of its time under the cover of rocks, logs, or vegetative litter. If caught by the tail, this skink tends to bite, and it may shed its tail to escape. Juveniles have a blue tail that turns brown or gray in adulthood. The tip of the tail and sides of the head are orange on breeding males. **Where found:** rocky areas in grasslands, shrublands, forests, and riparian areas; southern B.C., Idaho, western Montana, and north-central Utah.

Rubber Boa
Charina bottae
LENGTH: 14–33 in (35–84 cm)

Observing the rubber boa in its natural habitat is a rare experience. It is active from dusk until dawn hunting for lizards, amphibians, birds, and small mammals. Like most constrictors, the rubber boa is an excellent climber and it conquers its prey by strangling it. This species bears live young. Its short, stout, olive-green to brown body has cream or yellow undersides and a blunt, rounded tail. **Where found:** moist coniferous forests, meadows, and riparian areas; from southern B.C. and Alberta to Wyoming and Utah.

Yellow-bellied Racer
Coluber constrictor
LENGTH: 24–81 in (60–200 cm)

This large predator relies on speed to catch prey and escape danger. Most commonly seen on the ground, it will also climb shrubs to find birds and insects. It gets a better view of the terrain by moving with its head held above the ground. This slender snake is grayish or olive-green with green to bluish sides, yellow undersides, and a whip-like tail. The young have large, dark blotches or saddles on their backs and faint blotches on their sides. **Where found:** open forests, wooded hills, grassy ditches, and riparian areas; Idaho, western Montana, Utah, and western Colorado and may be found at lower elevations in Wyoming.

Western Smooth Green Snake
Opheodrys vernalis
LENGTH: 12–26 in (30–66 cm)

The coloration of this diurnal snake gives it superb camouflage among grasses, herbs, and shrubs, but after death its color quickly changes to bluish-gray. A number of female Western smooth green snakes may share a single nesting site, where each female lays 3–18 eggs. If you are lucky, you may find some of these lovely snakes sheltered under logs, rocks, or boards. **Where found:** moist meadows, rocky areas, forests, and riparian areas mainly in the foothills and montane zones; southeastern Idaho, south-central Wyoming, northeastern Utah, Colorado, and New Mexico.

Great Basin Gopher Snake
Pituophis catenifer
LENGTH: 3–8 ft (91–250 cm)

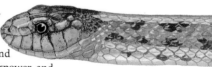

This large and beautiful constrictor is often mistaken for a rattlesnake owing to its similar coloration, patterning, and aggressive defensive strategy. When threatened, it hisses and vibrates its tail against vegetation, often producing a rattling sound. It frequently overwinters in communal dens with other snakes, including rattlesnakes, garter snakes, and racers. **Where found:** in a variety of forested and open habitats at lower elevations; from Alberta south. **Also known as:** bullsnake, pine-gopher snake.

Western Terrestrial Garter Snake
Thamnophis elegans
LENGTH: 17–41 in (45–105 cm)

Most garter snakes are primarily aquatic, hunting for food in or near sources of water, but the western terrestrial garter snake is not bound to watery habitats and will eat just about any animal it can overpower and swallow. When captured, it attempts to make itself unappetizing by secreting a foul-smelling liquid from its vent. **Where found:** low-elevation grasslands and shrublands to high-elevation meadows and forests; throughout the Rockies. **Also known as:** wandering garter snake.

Common Garter Snake
Thamnophis sirtalis
LENGTH: 20–51 in (50–130 cm)

Swift on land and in water, the common garter snake is an efficient hunter of amphibians, fish, small mammals, slugs, and leeches. A single female can give birth to 3–83 young in a single litter anytime between May and October. Their coloration varies from dark olive-green to black. The red-sided variety has red to orange blotches or a stripe on both sides. **Where found:** at lower elevations, in or close to water; common in B.C., Alberta, and Utah with population pockets in Wyoming, Colorado, and New Mexico. **Also known as:** red-sided garter snake, valley garter snake.

Western Rattlesnake
Crotalus viridis
LENGTH: 16–60 in (40–150 cm) long

The western rattlesnake is generally unappreciated by humans, but it serves a vital ecological role in preying upon small mammals. Bee venom is more toxic to humans than the venom of this snake—it is the larger dosage of snake venom that makes it more harmful. This tan to greenish-brown snake has facial pits between and below its eyes and nostrils. **Where found:** dry grasslands, shrublands, sagebrush, and rocky areas; from Montana and Idaho south. **Also known as:** prairie rattlesnake, midget-faded rattlesnake.

FISH

Fish are ectothermic vertebrates that live in the water, have streamlined bodies that are covered in scales, and possess fins and gills. A fundamental feature of fish is the serially repeated set of vertebrae and segmented muscles that allow the fish to move side to side thus propelling it through the water. A varying number of fins (depending on species) further aid the fish to swim and navigate. Rocky Mountain fish are oviparous: they lay eggs that are fertilized externally. Eggs are either produced in vast quantities and scattered, or they are laid in a spawning nest (redds) under rocks or logs. Parental care may be present in the defense of such a nest or territory. Spawning may involve migrating vast distances back to the freshwater spawning grounds after spending 2–3 years in the Pacific Ocean. Fish are an important food source for many animals in the Rocky Mountains.

Chinook Salmon

Oncorhynchus tshawytscha

LENGTH: 31–59 in (80–150 cm)

The chinook salmon is the largest North American salmon, weighing up to 126 lb (57 kg). Most salmon born in Idaho spend a year in freshwater, and then travel 900 mi (1448 km) to the Pacific Ocean. After 3 years in the ocean, they return to their place of birth to spawn and then die. During spawning, males have a slightly humped back and a hooked jaw, and they turn dark red to black with a greenish head. **Where found:** only in B.C. along the Fraser River and its tributaries in August and September and in Idaho along the south fork of the Salmon River. **Also known as:** king salmon, spring salmon, tyee.

Rainbow Trout
Oncorhynchus mykiss
LENGTH: 7½–18 in (19–46 cm)

Although native to much of western North America, this popular fish has been introduced worldwide. Both native and introduced populations are in the Rockies. Rainbow trout are an important food for animals such as mink and river otter. A form of rainbow trout called the 'steelhead' is born in freshwater rivers and streams, and migrates to the ocean like a salmon. When spawning, this trout changes color to have a greenish to bluish back, silvery sides and belly often tinged with yellow and green, and a reddish lateral line. **Where found:** lakes and streams at most elevations; throughout the Rockies.

Cutthroat Trout
Oncorhynchus clarki
LENGTH: 8–12 in (20–31 cm)

Named for the red streaking in the skin under the lower jaw, cutthroat trout seen in the water can be mistakenly identified as the similar-looking rainbow (above) or golden trout (below). Look for female cutthroats excavating their spawning nests (redds) with their tails in late spring or early summer. The reddish belly and throat become brighter during spawning. **Where found:** lakes and streams at most elevations; throughout the Rockies.

Golden Trout
Oncorhynchus aguabonita
LENGTH: 10¼–15 in (26–38 cm)

A strikingly beautiful fish, the golden trout has been stocked in many of the cold, azure-blue lakes of the Rocky Mountain alpine ecoregion. Females release bright orange eggs during mid-summer spawn; however, natural reproduction has been successful in only a few stocked lakes. **Where found:** introduced to high alpine lakes and streams; native distribution is limited to a few tributaries of the Kern River in California.

Lake Trout
Salvelinus namaycush
LENGTH: 20–47 in (51–120 cm)

The lake trout is a large freshwater
fish that feeds on invertebrates and fish, including min-
nows, suckers, and other trout. It is a slow-growing fish, but can live for over 20
years and grow to over 100 lb (45 kg)! The grayish-brown to olive-green back has
many light spots often forming into vermiculations. **Where found:** deep, cold
lakes where summer temperatures at lower depths are below 50° F (10° C); native
populations in B.C., Alberta, and Montana and introduced populations from B.C.
and Alberta south.

Bull Trout
Salvelinus confluentus
LENGTH: 7½–33 in (19–85 cm)

Recently distinguished from a
similar coastal species called the
Dolly Varden (*S. malma*), the bull trout is restricted to
the clean, cold waters of the Rockies. Bull trout spawn in September to October,
requiring cold streams with clean gravel in which to excavate their redds and lay
their eggs. Alberta populations of bull trout are increasingly threatened owing to
habitat loss, reduced water quality, siltation of spawning grounds, overfishing,
and competition with introduced brook trout. Light-colored spots on an olive-
green to gray-green body become pink to rosy-orange on spawing fish. **Where
found:** cold headwater streams and higher-elevation lakes; B.C., Alberta, Idaho,
and Montana. **Also known as:** mountain char.

Brook Trout
Salvelinus fontinalis
LENGTH: 10¼–30 in (26–76 cm)

Colorful and feisty, the
brook trout is a prized game fish
introduced from eastern North America. It is
known to interbreed with bull, lake, and brown trout.
Unfortunately, because of its interbreeding capabilities and preference for similar
foods, the brook trout is outcompeting some populations of native bull trout.
Where found: higher-elevation streams and lakes; throughout the Rockies.

Brown Trout
Salmo trutta
LENGTH: 18–35 in (46–89 cm)

The brown trout's large size and adaptability have made it a popular game fish throughout the world. Like most other trout, it spawns in fall and eats aquatic invertebrates. Brown trout will also eat the occasional amphibian or small mammal that ventures into the water. Color ranges from golden-brown to olive. This species was introduced to North America from Europe. **Where found:** streams, ponds, lakes, and reservoirs, usually at lower elevations; throughout the Rockies.

Mountain Whitefish
Prosopium williamsoni
LENGTH: 14–23 in (36–59 cm)

Popular among anglers, these members of the Trout Family live in fast-flowing mountain streams. They eat the aquatic larvae of insects and terrestrial insects caught in the cold water. Spawning females release up to 8000 eggs, which, when fertilized, sink to the bottom of the stream among sheltering crevices between rocks and gravel. **Where found:** streams and shallow areas of lakes; from B.C. and Alberta to Wyoming.

Arctic Grayling
Thymallus arcticus
LENGTH: 7¹/₂–20 in (19–50 cm)

This attractive fish is known for the male's large and colorful dorsal fin, which is draped over the female's back during spawning. Spawning occurs in the spring from March to June in cold, clear, unpolluted streams. Grayling can often be found feeding in schools. **Where found:** native habitat includes clear, cold streams and lakes; Alberta, B.C., Montana, and successfully introduced to Idaho and Wyoming.

Lake Chub
Couesius plumbeus
LENGTH: 2–4 in (5–10 cm)

These abundant minnows are
extremely important in Canadian mountain waters.
They eat a wide range of aquatic invertebrates and algae, and are in turn eaten by
larger fish and birds. In June and July they migrate upstream to cold mountain
headwaters to spawn. **Where found:** lakes, ponds, marshes, and streams from
lower elevations up to treeline; abundant throughout the Canadian Rockies, with
small populations in Montana and Idaho.

Longnose Dace
Rhinichthys cataractae
LENGTH: 3½–6½ in (9–17 cm)

Adapted for living along
the rocky bottoms of fast-
flowing mountain streams, the longnose
dace is benthic (bottom living). This minnow thrives
on the aquatic larvae of mosquitoes, midges, and other insects. A dark lateral band
is often present in young fish, and breeding males display a reddish-orange tinge
on their head, body, and fins. **Where found:** common in many different aquatic
habitats, including fast-flowing streams and cold- and warm-water springs and
lakes; throughout the Rockies.

Longnose Sucker
Catostomus catostomus
LENGTH: 17–25 in (43–64 cm)

These fish are bottom
feeders that eat worms,
crustaceans, mollusks, and
the aquatic larvae of insects. In May,
spawning males become spectacularly colored
in crimson-red and black. Large schools of young longnose suckers provide easy
meals for diving birds, such as the belted kingfisher and osprey. **Where found:**
rivers and lakes; from B.C. and Alberta to central Colorado.

INVERTEBRATES

There are hundreds of species of insects in the Rocky Mountains but the few mentioned in this guide are frequently encountered and easily recognizable. They provide food for birds, amphibians, shrews, bats, and other insects, and play an important role in the pollination of plants.

Ant
Order Hymenoptera
LENGTH: up to ¾ in (0.2–2 cm)

Ants represent one of the world's most successful faunal groups. Many species live in the Rocky Mountains. Ant colonies have one large, egg-producing queen, many sterile workers, and a few fertile winged males and females who fly to new areas to mate and form new colonies. Some ants will bite when threatened, creating a stinging effect by spraying the bitten area with formic acid stored in their abdomens. **Where found:** up to treeline; throughout the Rockies.

Mosquito
Order Diptera
LENGTH: ¼–½ in (0.3–1.3 cm)

The mosquito is annoying and unavoidable throughout the Rockies: there are approximately 30 known species in the Canadian Rockies alone. After mating, male mosquitos die and females collect blood, which is necessary for egg production and development. Eggs are laid in standing water or slow-moving streams. The maggot-like, aquatic larvae are food for many fish and predatory invertebrates, while adults are food for many birds, amphibians, and bats. **Where found:** everywhere—mainly from June to August, depending on elevation; throughout the Rockies.

Caddisfly
Order Trichoptera
LENGTH: up to 2 in (0.2–5 cm)

Caddisflies spend most of their lives as an aquatic larvae feeding on tiny aquatic plants and animals. Larvae can be found in standing and flowing waters where they feed fish, including the bull trout and diving birds, such as the American dipper. The caterpillar-like larvae are known for the diversely elaborate cases they make of pebbles, sand, silk, or plant material to protect their soft, vulnerable bodies. Flying adults appear in summer to find a mate and breed before dying. Adults are eaten by birds, amphibians, dragonflies, fish, and bats. **Where found:** most aquatic habitats; throughout the Rockies.

Dragonfly
Order Odonata

LENGTH: 1–3 in (2.5–8 cm)

Agile and deadly hunters of the air, dragonflies are a hiker's best friend. In addition to providing awe-inspiring aerial shows and flashes of brilliant color, these insects eat tremendous numbers of irritating biting insects, such as mosquitos and black flies. Both the aquatic larva and the aerial adult dragonflies possess voracious appetites. Many species of dragonfly can be easily identified by their colorful markings. **Where found:** marshes, ponds, marshy lakeshores, and slow-moving streams; numerous species throughout the Rockies.

Predaceous Diving Beetle
Order Coleoptera

LENGTH: 1/2–2 5/8 in (1.2–6.3 cm)

Equipped with a hard exoskeleton, large, efficient swimming limbs, and sharp, chewing mouthparts, this beetle is a ferocious and impressive aquatic hunter. Because it must breath atmospheric air, it dives with a bubble of air taken from the surface, allowing it to breath underwater. These beetles breed and lay their eggs on land, where the young pupate in damp forest soils before flying to water as adults. **Where found:** marshes, ponds, and slow-moving streams; many species of this beetle are throughout the Rockies.

Wood Tick
Order Acarina, *Dermacentor andersoni*

LENGTH: 1/4 in (5 mm)

The anti-coagulant fluid injected by a wood tick is **toxic** to the human nervous system. Symptoms such as numbness, drowsiness, lack of coordination, and even changes in personality have occurred from bites to the neck. These side-effects clear up shortly after the tick is removed. Ticks may also carry Rocky Mountain spotted fever that can cause severe illness and even death if left untreated. It is important to check your group for ticks after each day in the Rockies. Most ticks can be removed easily before they begin feeding. A feeding tick can be removed by pulling its body using a gentle, steady motion. **Where found:** most common during spring in short grasses and plants, at most elevations; throughout the Rockies.

Monarch Butterfly
Danaus plexippus
WINGSPAN: 3–4 in (8–10 cm)

The regal monarch butterfly is North America's most famous butterfly, known for its wide distribution and incredible migration. Millions of monarchs overwinter as adults in the mountain forests of southern California and Mexico. With warmer temperatures, adults migrate northward, laying eggs in patches of milkweed plants. These eggs quickly develop into adults, which continue north as far as the Canadian Rockies. Toxic compounds in the milkweed are ingested by monarch larvae and remain in both larvae and adults, making them unpalatable and toxic to birds and mammals. **Where found:** milkweed patches and flower meadows; throughout the Rockies.

Weidemeyer's Admiral
Limenitis weidemeyerii
WINGSPAN: 2½–3 in (6.5–7.6 cm)

These lovely butterflies typically fly from early June to late July, searching for tasty flower nectar and available mates. After mating, females deposit greenish eggs, each on its own leaf of willow, poplar, or saskatoon. Once hatched, young larvae feed briefly before building a leafy shelter in which to overwinter. Larvae resume their development the following spring until, as larger caterpillars, they are ready to pupate—their final metamorphosis into flying adult butterflies. Their wings are black with white dorsally and white with red and bluish patches ventrally. **Where found:** riparian areas and valley bottoms; from southern B.C. and Alberta south.

Mourning Cloak
Nymphalis antiopa
WINGSPAN: 2½–3 in (6–7.6 cm)

Adult mourning cloaks are one of the longest living butterflies, living for up to 10 months. Adults that take flight in July and August may overwinter in sheltered sites, re-emerging in spring to mate and lay eggs. Larvae are communal feeders, often defoliating large parts of host plants, including trembling aspen, American elm (*Ulmus americana*), and various willows. Adults fly at any time of the year in warmer parts of their range or during bouts of warm winter weather. **Where found:** at most elevations with trees and shrubs; throughout the Rockies.

Anise Swallowtail
Papilio zelicaon
WINGSPAN: 2⅝–3 in (6.5–8 cm)

The anise swallowtail is one of a number of radiant swallowtail butterfly species in the Rockies. Its larval hosts are usually members of the Carrot Family, including parsnips, parsleys, and angelicas. Adults may be seen from April to August, depending on the elevation and seasonal temperature. Like most butterflies, the anise swallowtail's wings have black coloration over the veins. The dark color absorbs solar energy, allowing the butterfly to quickly warm its body to flying temperature during cold mountain mornings. **Where found:** moist valley meadows to subalpine forests; throughout the Rockies.

Spring Azure
Celastrina argiolus
WINGSPAN: 1–1¼ in (2.5–3 cm)

A member of the dainty Blue Family of butterflies, the spring azure takes flight in early May, feeding on the buds and flowers of blooming mountain shrubs. It uses its fragile antennae to 'smell' and assist in providing balance. An adult lives to breed for only a few days before dying. Its larvae often develop on the leaves of red osier dogwood and choke cherry, and may be tended and protected by ants for the sweet 'honeydew' that caterpillars produce. **Where found:** lush valley bottoms to high alpine meadows; throughout the Rockies.

Clouded Sulphur
Colias philodice
WINGSPAN: 1½–2 in (3.8–5 cm)

Like all other butterflies, the common clouded sulphur plays a vital role in pollinating many wild plants of the Rockies. Attracted to flowers by their brilliantly colored petals, butterflies obtain a sweet burst of nectar by drinking with their long, coilable proboscis. During feeding, the butterflies are sprinkled with fine, sticky pollen, which they carry to the next plant, resulting in plant pollination. **Where found:** meadows, fields, and vegetated roadsides from low-elevation valleys to the subalpine; throughout the Rockies.

PLANTS

Plants belong to the Kingdom Plantae. They are autotrophic, which means that they produce their own food from inorganic materials through a process called photosynthesis. Plants are the basis of all food webs. They supply oxygen to the atmosphere, modify climates, and create and hold down soil. They disperse their seeds and pollen through carriers such as wind or animals. Fossil fuels come from ancient deposits of organic matter—largely that of plants. In this book, plants are separated into three categories: trees, shrubs, and herbs.

TREES

Trees are plants that have a woody trunk (generally only 1), they are long lived, and are normally taller than 16 ft (5 m). There are 2 types of trees: coniferous and deciduous. Trees are important to various ecosystems. A single tree can provide a home or a food source for many different animals. A group of trees can provide wind breaks and camouflage or shelter, hold down soil, or indicate water sources. A forest that is large and diverse in its structure and composition (species variety, understory, age, density, old-growth) defines the community of species that live within it. The integrity of a forest relies on having a large enough area and variety of plant species and ages. Old-growth forest is critical habitat for many species that use the fallen or hollowed out trees as nesting or denning sites. Many species of invertebrates live within or under the bark, providing food for birds. Fallen decomposing logs provide habitat for mosses, fungi, and invertebrates. The logs eventually completely degrade into nutrient-rich soil to perpetuate the continued growth of plant life and retain organic matter in the ecosystem. Large forests retain CO_2, an important preventive factor of global warming, and responsibly managed forests can sustain an industry that provides wood products and jobs.

BALSAM POPLAR
p. 116

TREMBLING ASPEN
p. 116

WHITE BIRCH
p. 117

PONDEROSA PINE
p. 117

LIMBER PINE
p. 118

LODGEPOLE PINE
p. 118

WESTERN LARCH
p. 119

DOUGLAS-FIR
p. 119

SUBALPINE FIR
p. 120

ENGELMANN SPRUCE
p. 120

WESTERN
HEMLOCK, p. 121

WESTERN
RED CEDAR, p. 121

Balsam Poplar
Populus balsamifera

HEIGHT: 33–82 ft (10–25 m)
LEAF LENGTH: 2–4¾ in (5–12 cm)
FEMALE CATKIN LENGTH: 1⅝–4 in (4–10 cm)
FRUITS: ¼–⅜ in (5–8 mm)

The trunks of these trees can obtain girths of up to 3½ ft (1 m) with bark becoming deeply furrowed and dark gray when old. This tree had several traditional uses in native medicines, as well as being a source of sugar, fragrance, ink, and tipi firewood. Ungulates browse on the young trees and bees collect the sticky, aromatic resin from the buds to cement and waterproof their hives. The male and female flowers are in catkins on separate trees and the white, tufted seeds disperse in large, fluffy masses. *P. trichocarpa* is a taller subspecies found in the southern half of the range and differentiated by variations in the catkins. **Where found:** moist to wet sites, often on river and lakeshores in foothills to subalpine zones from Colorado north. **Also known as:** black cottonwood.

Trembling Aspen
Populus tremuloides

HEIGHT: 33–66 ft (10–20 m)
LEAF LENGTH: ¾–3 in (2–8 cm)
CATKIN LENGTH: ¾–4 in (2–10 cm)

Suckers from the shallow, spreading roots of this deciduous tree can colonize many hectares of land. Single trunks are short lived, but a colony (clone) can survive for thousands of years. The greenish photosynthetic bark produces a white powder to protect the trees from ultraviolet radiation in open areas. This powder can be used as sunscreen. Long, slender, flattened stalks cause the leaves to 'tremble' in the breeze. The tiny fruits and flowers form slender, hanging clusters (catkins). **Where found:** dry to moist sites in foothills, montane, and subalpine zones throughout the Rockies.

White Birch
Betula papyrifera

HEIGHT: 33–66 ft (10–20 m)
LEAF LENGTH: 1½–3½ in (4–9 cm)
FEMALE CATKIN LENGTH: 2–4 in (5–10 cm)

These attractive, fast-growing deciduous trees often grace parks and yards. They frequently grow in clumps, because damaged trees re-sprout several trunks. Native peoples used the thin, paper-like bark to make baskets, cups, and platters, and the hard wood to make sleds, snowshoes, paddles, and even needles. Do not remove sheets of bark—it can permanently scar and even kill a tree. The egg-shaped leaves turn yellow in fall. The tiny flowers and fruits form dense, elongated catkins. **Where found:** a wide range of sites, from foothills to subalpine zones; from Colorado north. **Also known as:** paper birch.

Ponderosa Pine
Pinus ponderosa

HEIGHT: 33–130 ft (10–40 m)
NEEDLE LENGTH: 4–10 in (10–25 cm)
SEED CONE LENGTH: 3–5½ in (8–14 cm)

These stately pines thrive in areas that are periodically burned. Their straight, cinnamon-colored trunks are distinctive: black fissures outline a jigsaw puzzle of thick plates of bark. Native peoples ground the oil-rich seeds into meal. They also collected the sweet inner bark in spring, when the sap was running. Large scars still remain on some older trees, attesting to people's fondness for this sweet treat. The needles are in bundles of three and the cones have thick, dull brown scales tipped with a stiff prickle. **Where found:** dry sites in foothills and montane zones; from southern B.C. south. **Also known as:** yellow pine.

Limber Pine

Pinus flexilis

HEIGHT: 13–50 ft (4–15 m)
NEEDLE LENGTH: 1⅝–2¾ in (4–7 cm)
SEED CONE LENGTH: 2–4¾ in (5–12 cm)

Gnarled, twisted limber pine trees can cling tenaciously to exposed bluffs and cliffs for over 1000 years. Native peoples and settlers followed the example of local birds, small mammals, and grizzly bears, collecting the nutritious, oil-rich seeds of this coniferous evergreen for food. The name *flexilis* refers to the flexible branches, a necessary adaptation for survival under such windy conditions. The seed (female) cones have thick scales with no prickles. Western white pine (*P. monticola*) has thin-scaled, long-stalked, cylindrical cones and soft, finely toothed needles. **Where found:** warm ridges and rocky slopes in foothills, montane, and subalpine zones; from B.C. and Alberta south.

Lodgepole Pine

Pinus contorta

HEIGHT: 6½–82 ft (2–25 m)
NEEDLE LENGTH: ¾–2½ in (2–6 cm)
SEED CONE LENGTH: ¾–2½ in (2–6 cm)

Dense, pure stands of this tall, slender pine grow quickly after fire, and blanket large sections of the Rockies. The cones are sealed with resin, but this resin is melted by heat, releasing the stock-piled seed. Young stands can have over 100,000 trees per hectare. The straight, slender trunks were used to construct travois, tipis, and cabins—hence the name lodgepole pine. **Where found:** moist to dry sites in foothills and montane zones; from Colorado north.

Western Larch
Larix occidentalis

HEIGHT: 82–165 ft (25–50 m)
NEEDLE LENGTH: 1–2 in (2.5–5 cm)
SEED CONE LENGTH: 1–1⅝ in (2.5–4 cm)

These slender, exotic-looking trees differ from most conifers in that their leaves turn bright yellow and drop in autumn. The sap contains the natural sugar gelatin, and native peoples collected it and the sweet inner bark in spring. Lumps of pitch were chewed like gum. Thick bark helps mature trees to survive fires, and some live for 700–900 years. The soft needles are pale yellow-green and grow in tufts of 15–30 on stubby twigs. Subalpine larch (*L. lyallii*), has wooly (rather than almost hairless) young twigs and grows at higher elevations. **Where found:** gravelly, wet sites in upper foothills and montane zones; from B.C. and Alberta to Oregon and Montana.

Douglas-fir
Pseudotsuga menziesii

HEIGHT: 82–130 ft (25–40 m)
NEEDLE LENGTH: ¾–1¼ in (2–3 cm)
SEED CONE LENGTH: 2–4 in (5–10 cm)

This common evergreen with its compact, pyramidal crowns and (often) drooping branches is one of the world's best-known timber-producers. With their thick, 3–8 in (8–20 cm), fire-resistant bark and shade-tolerance, Douglas-firs can live for well over 1000 years. In native myths, mice once hid in these cones—you can still see their tails and hind legs, sticking out from under the scales. The aromatic needles are flat, blunt, and often flattened in 2 rows. **Where found:** moist to very dry sites in foothills, montane, and subalpine zones; from B.C. and Alberta south.

Subalpine Fir
Abies bifolia; A. lasiocarpa

HEIGHT: 66–100 ft (20–30 m)
NEEDLE LENGTH: ¾–1⅝ in (2–4 cm)
SEED CONE LENGTH: 2–4 in (5–10 cm)

The fragrance of these resinous evergreens often permeates the air near treeline. In sheltered valleys the spire-like crowns can reach their maximum height, but on high, exposed slopes trees grow stunted and twisted like bonsai. Native peoples used powdered fir needles as baby powder and body scent, and mixed it with grease to make hair tonic and salves. Fir incense was burned to repel evil spirits. The needles are flat and blunt and the smooth bark has resin blisters. **Where found:** subalpine slopes; from northern Canada south.

Engelmann Spruce
Picea engelmannii

HEIGHT: 82–100 ft (25–30 m)
NEEDLE LENGTH: ¾–1¼ in (2–3 cm)
SEED CONE LENGTH: 1⅝–2 in (4–5 cm)

Narrow, spire-like crowns, whorls of drooping lower branches, and sharp, 4-sided needles help to identify this common, aromatic evergreen. Native peoples made canoes from the bark, and split the roots to make cord and thread. The strong, uniform wood is used for lumber, plywood, poles, and railway ties. In the Canadian Rockies, white spruce (*P. glauca*) trees are widespread. They are recognized by the rounded (not wavy) cone scales, but hybrids of these 2 species can make identification difficult. **Where found:** cool, moist slopes in montane and subalpine zones; from B.C. and Alberta south.

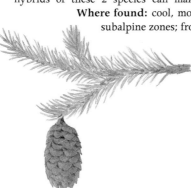

Western Hemlock
Tsuga heterophylla
HEIGHT: 100–165 ft (30–50 m)
NEEDLE LENGTH: 3/8–3/4 in (0.8–2 cm)
SEED CONE LENGTH: 5/8–1 in (1.5–2.5 cm)

These attractive, feathery trees are popular as ornamentals. The hard, strong, even-grained wood is widely used to make cabinets, moldings, and floors, and provides lumber, pilings, poles, and pulp. The crushed needles were thought to smell like poison-hemlock plants, hence the common name. The needles are flat, blunt, unequal, and in 2 opposite rows. In subalpine zones, mountain hemlock (*T. mertensiana*) has cones that are 2–3 times as long as those of western hemlock and needles in a bottlebrush-like arrange- ment (not 2 rows). **Where found:** moist sites in foothills and montane zones; in B.C., Alberta, Idaho, and Montana.

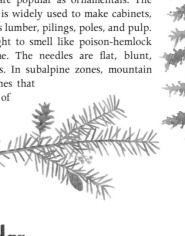

Western Red Cedar
Thuja plicata
HEIGHT: up to 130 ft (40 m)
SEED CONE LENGTH: less than 1/2 in (0.8–1.2 cm)

These majestic, coniferous trees can live for over 1000 years. Native peoples twisted, wove, and plaited long, soft strings of the inner bark to make baskets, blankets, clothing, ropes, and mats. The light, soft, aromatic wood splits easily and resists decay. Today, it is widely used for siding, roofing, doors, and patio furniture. The seed (female) cones have 6–8 brown scales and are born near the tips of flattened sprays of scale- like leaves. **Where found:** moist, rich sites in foothills and montane forests; from B.C. to southern Alberta to Idaho.

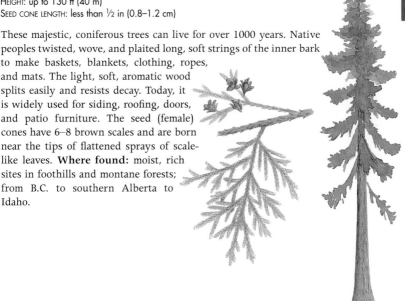

SHRUBS

Shrubs survive several seasons and are therefore called perennials. They have 1 or more woody stems, are normally less than 16 ft (5 m) tall, or they may be a vine. Several shrubs flower and often produce fruit—commonly called berries. These low-growth forms provide beneficial habitat and shelter. Their berries, leaves, and often bark are crucial food sources and provide forage for many animals. The tasty berries of several shrubs have been a staple of native and traditional foods and they are still enjoyed by people throughout the Rocky Mountain region. The shrubs illustrated here are the first representatives of each group as they appear in this guide.

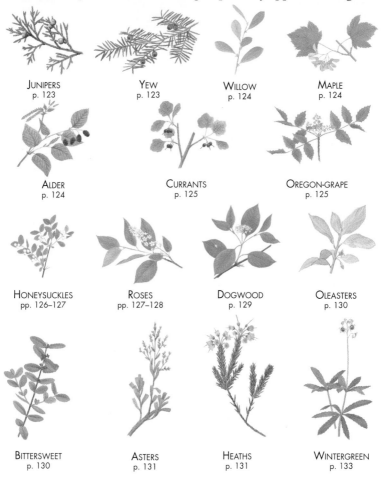

JUNIPERS
p. 123

YEW
p. 123

WILLOW
p. 124

MAPLE
p. 124

ALDER
p. 124

CURRANTS
p. 125

OREGON-GRAPE
p. 125

HONEYSUCKLES
pp. 126–127

ROSES
pp. 127–128

DOGWOOD
p. 129

OLEASTERS
p. 130

BITTERSWEET
p. 130

ASTERS
p. 131

HEATHS
p. 131

WINTERGREEN
p. 133

Rocky Mountain Juniper
Juniperus scopulorum

HEIGHT: 3½–33 ft (1–10 m) tall
LEAF LENGTH: less than ⅛ in (1–1.5 mm)
POLLEN CONE LENGTH: less than ¼ in (5 mm)

These cedar-like shrubs dot dry hillsides at lower elevations.
Native peoples used the tough wood to make bows, clubs, and utensils, and the aromatic leaves and berries to treat many ailments, but like common juniper, this shrub can be **toxic**. The tiny, scale-like leaves are sometimes needle-like when young. The egg-shaped pollen (male) cones and the smaller grayish-purple, berry-like seed (female) cones are borne on separate shrubs. A low-growing relative, creeping juniper (*J. horizontalis)*, has trailing branches less than 6 in (15 cm) high.
Where found: dry, rocky foothills and montane slopes; from B.C. and Alberta south.

Common Juniper
Juniperus communis

HEIGHT: 1–3½ ft (30–100 cm)
NEEDLE LENGTH: ¼–½ in (0.5–1.2 cm)
SEED CONE LENGTH: ⅜–½ in (0.8–1.2 cm)

The blue-gray 'berries' are in fact tiny cones with 3–8 fleshy scales. They can add spice to food and flavoring to gin, but pregnant women and people with kidney problems should never use them. Europeans made juniper berry tea to treat eating disorders, diarrhea, and heart, lung, and kidney problems. Native peoples burned juniper branches to purify homes, protect people from evil, and bring good luck to hunters. This pungent, prickly, clumped, or matted evergreen produces pollen (male) and seed (female) cones on separate shrubs. **Where found:** dry, open sites in plains to alpine zones; throughout the Rockies.

Western Yew
Taxus brevifolia

HEIGHT: 16–33 ft (5–10 m)
NEEDLE LENGTH: about ⅝ in (14–18 mm)
FRUIT WIDTH: less than ¼ in (4–5 mm)
CONE LENGTH: less than ⅛ in (2–3 mm)

Dark, flat evergreen needles and bright scarlet berries make this an attractive, drooping, ornamental shrub, but all parts are **poisonous**. Birds eat the fruits, and moose seek out the shrubs for winter food. The bark contains taxol, a drug used to treat ovarian and breast cancer. The heavy, fine-grained wood is prized by carvers for its with purplish-red, papery bark over rose-colored inner bark. The flowers are borne in tiny cones. **Where found:** moist, shady sites in foothills and montane zones; from B.C. and Alberta to Idaho and Montana.

Scouler's Willow
Salix scouleriana

HEIGHT: 6½–30 ft (2–9 m)
LEAF LENGTH: 1¼–4 in (3–10 cm)
CATKIN LENGTH: ¾–1⅝ in (2–4 cm)
FRUIT LENGTH: ¼–⅜ in (5–8 mm)

Willows are extremely common, but it is often hard to identify each species. Dense, elongating flower clusters (catkins) and buds covered by a single scale identify this group. Scouler's willow is a spindly, clumped, deciduous shrub with short, stiff, rust-colored hairs on the undersides of its leaves. The seed (female) catkins appear before the leaves and produce long-beaked, short-stalked, hairy capsules containing tiny, silky-tufted seeds. Bebb's willow (*S. bebbiana*) is a 3½–16 ft (1–5 m) tall species, with slender, long-stalked capsules and with a raised network of veins on the lower surface of young leaves. **Where found:** moist to wet sites in foothills and montane zones; throughout the Rockies.

Rocky Mountain Maple
Acer glabrum

HEIGHT: 3½–23 ft (1–7 m)
LEAF WIDTH: ¾–4 in (2–10 cm)
FRUIT LENGTH: 1 in (2.5 cm)

With their broad maple-leaves and reddish clusters of keys, these small, clumped, deciduous shrubs are popular ornamentals. In autumn, they produce the first splashes of crimson in the forest. V-shaped pairs of wrinkled, winged seeds (keys) hang in clusters. Native peoples used the tough, pliable wood to make arrows, snowshoes, and implements. **Where found:** moist, sheltered sites in foothills and montane woods; from B.C. and Alberta south.

Green Alder
Alnus viridis; A crispa

HEIGHT: 3½–13 ft (1–4 m)
LEAF LENGTH: 1⅝–3 in (4–8 cm)
FEMALE CATKIN LENGTH: ½–⅝ in (1–1.5 cm)
MALE CATKIN LENGTH: 1¼–3 in (3–8 cm)

These tall, clumped deciduous shrubs were an important main fuel for smoking fish, meat, and hides. The twigs and inner bark produce a red dye that was used to color hides and fishnets. The fruits are tiny, broadly winged nutlets, shed from woody, egg-shaped clusters (female catkins). Tiny flowers form male or female catkins. By lakes and rivers, mountain alder (*A. incana*; *A. tenuifolia*) is distinguished by its dull green, wavy-lobed, doubly toothed leaves. **Where found:** streamsides and moist woods in foothills, montane, and subalpine zones; from Colorado north.

Squaw Currant
Ribes cereum

HEIGHT: 1½–5 ft (50–150 cm)
LEAF WIDTH: ³⁄₈–1⅝ in (1–4 cm)
FLOWER LENGTH: less than ³⁄₈ in (8 mm)
FRUIT WIDTH: ¼ in (6 mm)

These tasteless to bitter, glandular berries (currants) were
eaten only occasionally by native peoples. Some considered
them a tonic, or ate them to relieve diarrhea. The usually sticky-hairy, tubular flowers hang in clusters of 1–8, and are an important source of nectar for hummingbirds
early in the year. The species name *cereum* means 'waxy,' in reference to the waxy
appearance of the glandular, often sticky-hairy leaves. **Where found:** dry sites on
plains, foothills, and montane slopes; from B.C. south. **Also known as:** wax
currant.

Bristly Black Currant
Ribes lacustre

HEIGHT: 1½–5 ft (50–150 cm)
LEAF WIDTH: 1¼–1⅝ in (3–4 cm)
FLOWER WIDTH: ¼ in (6 mm)
FRUIT WIDTH: ¼–³⁄₈ in (5–8 mm)

Many native groups ate these edible (but insipid) berries, fresh or
cooked. Today, bristly black currants are usually made into jam. The branch spines
of this deciduous shrub cause serious **allergic** reactions in sensitive people, and
some groups considered the branches (and by extension, the bristly, glandular fruit)
to be **poisonous**. Wild currants are the intermediate host for blister rust, a virulent
disease of native 5-needled pines. The small flowers are reddish to maroon, hanging
in clusters of 7–15. **Where found:** moist, wooded, or open sites in foothills to
alpine zones; from northern Canada to Colorado.

Creeping Oregon-grape
Mahonia repens; Berberis repens

HEIGHT: 4–12 in (10–30 cm)
LEAFLET LENGTH: 1¼–3 in (3–8 cm)
FLOWER WIDTH: less than ½ in (1 cm)
FRUIT LENGTH: less than ³⁄₈ in (7–8 mm)

These small, low-growing wintergreen shrubs look like holly plants with grapes.
The spiny-toothed, leathery leaflets turn red or purple in winter. The juicy berries
are purplish-blue with a whitish bloom. Although the berries are sour, they can
be eaten raw, and they make good jelly, jam, and wine. The sweetened juice tastes
much like grape juice. These plants are good evergreens for gardens, and their red
and green winter leaves make attractive Christmas decorations. **Where found:**
wooded sites on foothills and montane slopes; from southern B.C. and Alberta
south.

Common Snowberry
Symphoricarpos albus

HEIGHT: 1½–2½ ft (50–75 cm)
LEAF LENGTH: ¾–1⅝ in (2–4 cm)
FLOWER LENGTH: ⅛–¼ in (4–7 mm)
FRUIT WIDTH: ¼–½ in (0.6–1 cm)

The name 'snowberry' refers to the waxy, white, berry-like drupes that remain in small clusters near branch tips through winter. All parts of these deciduous shrubs are **toxic**, causing vomiting and diarrhea. Some native groups called the fruits 'corpse berries,' because they were believed to be the ghosts of saskatoons—part of the spirit world, not to be eaten by the living. The broadly funnel-shaped flowers are pink to white and have hairy centers. Mountain snowberry (*S. oreophilus*) has ¼–½ in (0.7–1.2 cm) long, more tubular flowers. **Where found:** well-drained sites from the plains to lower subalpine zones; from B.C. and Alberta to Colorado.

Utah Honeysuckle
Lonicera utahensis

HEIGHT: 1½–6½ ft (50–200 cm)
LEAF LENGTH: ¾–2 in (2–5 cm)
FLOWER LENGTH: ½–¾ in (1–2 cm)
FRUIT WIDTH: ¼–⅜ in (6–8 mm)

These common, deciduous shrubs are easily propagated from cuttings and their delicate, yellow flowers or translucent, scarlet berries make them attractive ornamentals. The juicy berries are joined at the base in pairs. Hummingbirds and moths pollinate the flowers, as they hover and collect nectar, but unscrupulous nectar-robbing bees simply puncture the short spur at the flower's base and steal a meal. **Where found:** moist, wooded, or open sites in foothills and montane zones; from southern B.C. and Alberta to Utah and Wyoming.

Bracted Honeysuckle
Lonicera involucrata

HEIGHT: 3½–6½ ft (1–2 m)
FLOWER LENGTH: ½–¾ in (1–2 cm)
FRUIT WIDTH: less than ⅜ in (8 mm)

The unusual, shiny berries of these deciduous shrubs, with their broad, spreading, backward-bending, shiny red to purplish bracts, catch the eyes of passers-by and also of hungry bears and birds. Despite their tempting appearance, these berries are unpalatable and they can be **toxic**. **Where found:** moist to wet, usually shaded sites in foothills, montane, and subalpine zones; from B.C. and Alberta south.

Black Elderberry

Sambucus racemosa

HEIGHT: 3½–10 ft (1–3 m)
LEAFLET LENGTH: 2–6 in (5–15 cm)
FLOWER WIDTH: ⅛–¼ in (3–6 mm)
FRUIT WIDTH: less than ¼ in (5–6 mm)

Large, showy clusters of flowers or heavy, wide, berry-like drupes draw attention to this strong-smelling, clumped deciduous shrub. The berries can be made into jam, jelly, pies, and wine, but they are unpalatable and even **toxic** when raw or immature. The rest of the plant is **poisonous** to humans, though moose, deer, and elk seem to enjoy it. **Where found:** moist sites in foothills, montane, and subalpine zones; from B.C. and Alberta south.

Choke Cherry

Prunus virginiana

HEIGHT: 3½–16 ft (1–5 m)
LEAF LENGTH: 1¼–4 in (3–10 cm)
FLOWER WIDTH: about ½ in (1–1.2 cm)
FRUIT WIDTH: less than ⅜ in (8 mm)

This deciduous shrub has erect, 2–6 in (5–15 cm) long, bottlebrush-like clusters of flowers and hanging clusters of shiny drupes. Many native groups cooked these astringent, dark red or black cherries or dried them for use in pemmican or stews. Large quantities were pulverized with rocks, formed into patties, and dried. Today, choke cherries are made into jellies, syrups, sauces, and wines. Pin cherry (*P. pensylvanica*) has small, flat-topped clusters of ⅛–¼ in (4–7 mm) red cherries. All parts of both shrubs (except the cherry flesh) contain **poisonous** hydrocyanic acid. **Where found:** dry to moist slopes in plains, foothills, and montane zones; from southern NWT south.

Saskatoon

Amelanchier alnifolia

HEIGHT: 3½–16 ft (1–5 m)
LEAF LENGTH: ¾–2 in (2–5 cm)
FLOWER WIDTH: ¾ in (2 cm)
FRUIT WIDTH: ¼–½ in (0.6–1.2 cm)

Many native groups gathered these sweet, juicy 'berries.' Large quantities were dried (loose or in cakes) and mixed with meat and fat, or added to stews. Today, saskatoons are used in pies, pancakes, muffins, jams, jellies, syrups, and wine. The purple to black berries are actually small pomes. These hardy deciduous shrubs or small trees are easily propagated. They have beautiful white blossoms in spring, delicious fruit in summer, and scarlet leaves in autumn. **Where found:** open to wooded slopes in plains, foothills, and montane zones; throughout the Rockies.

Birch-leaved Spiraea

Spiraea betulifolia; S. lucida

HEIGHT: 16–28 in (40–70 cm)
LEAF LENGTH: ¾–2¾ in (2–7 cm)
FLOWER WIDTH: less than ¼ in (5 mm)
FRUIT LENGTH: ⅛ in (3 mm)

These attractive deciduous shrubs are easily overlooked, but when they bloom their showy white to purplish, 1¼–3 in (3–8 cm) wide flower clusters catch the eye of passers-by. Each flower has 5 tiny petals and 25–50 long stamens. Birch-leaved spiraea is hardy and easily grown from cuttings, or off shoots or seeds, but once established, it spreads rapidly by rhizomes, and can become difficult to control. Blue grouse eat young spiraea leaves, and deer browse on the shrubs. The fruits are pod-like capsules joined at the base in clusters of 5 per flower. **Where found:** moist slopes in foothills, montane, and subalpine zones from B.C. and Alberta to Wyoming.

Thimbleberry

Rubus parviflorus

HEIGHT: 1½–6½ ft (50–200 cm)
LEAF WIDTH: 2–8 in (5–20 cm)
FLOWER WIDTH: 1–2 in (2.5–5 cm)
FRUIT WIDTH: ⅝–¾ in (1.5–2 cm)

These beautiful, satiny raspberries are seedy and difficult to collect, but most native peoples ate them fresh from the bush because they are so common. Thimbleberries can be tasteless, tart or sweet, depending on the season and the site, but birds and bears always seem to enjoy them. Young shoots were also eaten, and the broad, 2–8 in (5–20 cm) wide leaves provided temporary plates, containers, and basket liners. This deciduous shrub, without prickles, often forms dense thickets. **Where found:** moist to dry sites in foothills and montane zones; from B.C. and Alberta south.

Prickly Rose

Rosa acicularis

HEIGHT: 8 in–4 ft (20–120 cm)
FLOWER WIDTH: 2–2¾ in (5–7 cm)
FRUIT LENGTH: ⅝–1¼ in (1.5–3 cm)

Because of their dense prickles and slender thorns, these sweet-smelling deciduous shrubs, with their fragrant pink roses and scarlet, berry-like hips are usually considered a nuisance. Prairie rose (*R. woodsii*) has smaller, ¼–½ in (0.6–1.2 cm) long, round hips, and only a few large thorns. Most parts of rose shrubs are edible, but the sweet, nutritious hips are eaten most commonly. Avoid the seeds; their sliver-like hairs can irritate the digestive tract and cause 'itchy bum.' **Where found:** dry to moist sites in plains to subalpine zones; throughout the Rockies.

Western Mountain-ash

Sorbus scopulina

HEIGHT: 3½–13 ft (1–4 m)
LEAFLET LENGTH: 1¼–2½ in (3–6 cm)
FLOWER WIDTH: less than ½ in (1 cm)
FRUIT LENGTH: less than ⅜ in (7–8 mm)

Deep green, glossy leaves and showy clusters of white flowers or glossy, berry-like pomes make western mountain-ash an attractive deciduous garden shrub. The juicy berries also attract many birds, and they last well as decorations. Some native peoples ate these bitter fruits, fresh or dried, but many considered them inedible. Today, they are sometimes made into jams and jellies. **Where found:** moist sites in foothills, montane, and subalpine zones; from northern Canada south.

Shrubby Cinquefoil

Pentaphylloides floribunda; Potentilla fruticosa

HEIGHT: 4–51 in (10–130 cm)
LEAFLET LENGTH: ½–¾ in (1–2 cm)
FLOWER WIDTH: ⅝–1¼ in (1.5–3 cm)

This hardy, deciduous shrub is widely used in gardens and public places. It is often covered with bright yellow blooms from spring to fall. Shrubby cinquefoil also provides erosion control, especially along highways. Heavily browsed cinquefoils indicate overgrazing, as most animals prefer other plants. The papery, shredding bark provided tinder for fires started by sparks or twirling sticks. The tiny fruits are light brown, hairy achenes. **Where found:** wet to dry, often rocky sites in plains to subalpine zones; throughout the Rockies.

Red-osier Dogwood

Cornus sericea; C. stolonifera

HEIGHT: 1½–10 ft (50–300 cm)
LEAF LENGTH: ¾–4 in (2–10 cm)
FLOWER WIDTH: less than ¼ in (5 mm)
FRUIT WIDTH: about ¼ in (5–7 mm)

This attractive, hardy, deciduous shrub has distinctive purple to red branches with white flowers in spring, red leaves in autumn, and white berry-like drupes in winter. It is easily grown from cuttings. Native peoples smoked the dried inner bark alone or with tobacco or common bearberry (kinnikinnick). The flexible branches were often woven into baskets, especially as decorative red rims. The bitter, juicy berries, mixed with sweeter fruit or sugar, made sweet-and-sour. **Where found:** moist sites in plains, foothills, and montane zones; from northern Canada south.

Silverberry
Elaeagnus commutata

HEIGHT: 3½–16 ft (1–5 m)
LEAF LENGTH: ¾–4 ft (2–10 cm)
FLOWER LENGTH: ½–⅝ in (1.2–1.6 cm)
FRUIT LENGTH: less than ½ in (1 cm)

Sweet, heavy perfume from the inconspicuous flowers of silvery wolfwillow colonies either delights or nauseates passers-by. Burning green wood gives off a strong smell of human excrement, an unpleasant surprise for some campers. The dry, mealy berries are edible, but not very palatable. They can be boiled to remove the flesh, and softened inner nutlets are then threaded, dried, oiled, and polished as decorative beads. The silvery leaves are covered in tiny star-shaped hairs. **Where found:** well-drained, open slopes in plains, foothills, and montane zones; from Idaho and Montana north. **Also known as:** wolfwillow.

Canada Buffaloberry
Shepherdia canadensis

HEIGHT: 3½–6½ ft (1–2 m)
LEAF LENGTH: ⅝–2½ in (1.5–6 cm)
FLOWER WIDTH: ⅛ in (4 mm)
FRUIT LENGTH: ⅛–¼ in (4–6 mm)

These tempting, juicy, translucent red berries are quite sour, but many native peoples enjoyed them. Buffaloberries contain a bitter, soapy substance (saponin) that foams when beaten. They were whipped like egg-whites to make a foamy dessert called Indian ice cream, which was sweetened with other berries, and later with sugar. This deciduous shrub has dark green, silvery leaves with star-shaped hairs and rust-colored scales. The inconspicuous, yellowish to greenish flowers are either male or female (on separate plants). **Where found:** open woods and stream-banks in foothills, montane, and subalpine zones; throughout the Rockies. **Also known as:** soopolallie.

Falsebox
Paxistima myrsinites; Pachistima myrsinites

HEIGHT: 8–24 in (20–60 cm)
LEAF LENGTH: ½–1¼ in (1–3 cm)
FLOWER WIDTH: ⅛ in (4 mm)
FRUIT LENGTH: ⅛ in (4 mm)

The glossy, stiff, leathery leaves of these low, branched, evergreen shrubs blanket the floor of many mountain forests. Sprays of falsebox are often used in flower arrangements, and over-collecting has depleted many populations. The greenish-brown to dark reddish flowers are borne in small clusters in the leaf axils. The fruits are oval capsules. To remember this unusual name, just repeat 'Pa kissed ma.' **Where found:** moist forests to well-drained, open sites in foothills, montane, and subalpine zones; from southern B.C. and Alberta south. **Also known as:** mountain boxwood.

Big Sagebrush

Artemisia tridentata

HEIGHT: 1½–6½ ft (50–200 cm)
LEAF LENGTH: ½–¾ in (1–2 cm)
FLOWERHEAD WIDTH: ½–2¾ in (1.5–7 cm)

These common shrubs, with sage-like aroma and grayish, shredding bark, have been used in a wide variety of medicines and were also burned as smudges and fumigants. Big sagebrush is a valuable food for many wild birds and mammals, but livestock avoid it. Antelopebrush or bitterbrush (*Purshia tridentata*) has very similar (though not aromatic) leaves, but it has small, bright yellow, rose-like flowers and velvety, about ⅝ in (1.5 cm) long, spindle-shaped, seed-like fruits. **Where found:** often covering many acres of dry plains and slopes; from southern B.C. and Alberta south.

Common Rabbitbush

Chrysothamnus nauseosus

HEIGHT: 8–24 in (20–60 cm)
LEAF LENGTH: 1¼–2½ in (3–6 cm)
FLOWERHEAD WIDTH: less than ¼ in (5 mm)

In late summer, these flat-topped, deciduous shrubs cover dry slopes with splashes of yellow. Native peoples made medicinal teas from the roots or leaves to treat coughs, colds, fevers, and menstrual pain. The dense branches were used to cover and carpet sweathouses, and they were burned slowly to smoke hides. Boiled flowerheads produced a lemon-yellow dye for wool, leather, and baskets. The flowers grow in clusters and the leaves are velvety. **Where found:** dry, open areas on plains, foothills, and montane zones; from southern B.C. and Alberta south.

Pink Mountain-heather

Phyllodoce empetriformis

HEIGHT: 4–8 in (10–20 cm)
LEAF LENGTH: ¼–½ in (0.5–1.2 cm)
FLOWER LENGTH: ¼–⅜ in (5–8 mm)
FRUIT WIDTH: ⅛ in (4 mm)

These bright, rose-pink clusters of tiny bells on deep green mats delight hikers across alpine slopes. Mountain-heather could be mistaken for crowberry (*Empetrum nigrum*), but crowberry has shorter leaves, inconspicuous flowers, and juicy black berries (rather than dry capsules). Needle-like leaves help these ground-hugging plants to survive in areas where frozen soil and cold, dry winds limit water. The fruits are erect, round capsules and the young shrub is glandular-hairy. **Where found:** moist to wet slopes in subalpine and alpine zones; from northern Canada to Idaho, Montana, and possibly Colorado.

Common Bearberry
Arctostaphylos uva-ursi

HEIGHT: 2–6 in (5–15 cm)
LEAF LENGTH: ½–1¼ in (1–3 cm)
FLOWER LENGTH: ⅛–¼ in (4–6 mm)
FRUIT WIDTH: ¼–½ in (0.6–1 cm)

Thick, leathery evergreen leaves help this common, mat-forming shrub to survive on dry, sunny slopes where others would perish. The 'berries' (berry-like drupes) are edible, but rather mealy and tasteless. They were cooked and mixed with grease or fish eggs, to reduce their dryness. The glossy leaves were widely used for smoking, both alone and later with tobacco. Trailing, 1½–3½ ft (50–100 cm) long branches send down roots, and the flowers nod in small clusters. **Where found:** well-drained, open, or wooded sites in foothills to alpine zones; throughout the Rockies. **Also known as:** kinnikinnick.

Grouseberry
Vaccinium scoparium

HEIGHT: 4–8 in (10–20 cm)
LEAF LENGTH: ¼–½ in (0.6–1.2 cm)
FLOWER LENGTH: ⅛ in (3 mm)
FRUIT WIDTH: ⅛–¼ in (3–5 mm)

It could take hours to collect even a small quantity of these tiny, sweet, red berries, but some natives gathered them using combs. Many birds and small mammals enjoy whortleberries. Grouse eat all parts of this small deciduous shrub—hence, 'grouseberry.' The small, thin leaves and dense, strongly angled, broom-like branches often form lacy mats. Another common species with shiny, toothed leaves, dwarf blueberry (*V. caespitosum*), has brownish branches that are neither distinctly angled nor broom-like. **Where found:** open or wooded sites in foothills, montane, and subalpine zones; from B.C. and Alberta to Colorado. **Also known as:** whortleberry.

Black Huckleberry
Vaccinium membranaceum; V. globulare

HEIGHT: 1–5 ft (30–150 cm)
LEAF LENGTH: ¾–2 in (2–5 cm)
FLOWER LENGTH: ¼ in (5–6 mm)
FRUIT WIDTH: ¼–½ in (0.7–1 cm)

Black huckleberries are among our most delicious and highly prized berries. Large quantities are collected in open, subalpine sites (such as old burns), and in some areas they are sold commercially. Native peoples ate them fresh, sun-dried, or smoke-dried for winter use (either loose or mashed and formed into cakes). Today, huckleberries are made into jams and jellies, or used in pancakes, muffins, and desserts. The finely toothed, deciduous leaves turn red or purple in autumn. **Where found:** moist, open sites in foothills and montane zones; from the southern NWT to Wyoming.

False Azalea
Menziesia ferruginea; M. glabella

HEIGHT: 1½–6½ ft (50–200 cm)
LEAF LENGTH: 1¼–2½ in (3–6 cm)
FLOWER LENGTH: about ¼ (6–8 mm)
FRUIT LENGTH: ¼ in (5–7 mm)

This deciduous shrub is sometimes called fool's huckleberry, because it looks like a huckleberry, but its fruit is a dry capsule. Like many members of the Heath Family, it contains the **poison** andromedotoxin. When not in flower, false azalea could be mistaken for white-flowered rhododendron (*Rhododendron albiflorum*), but rhododendron leaves are glossier, and their midveins do not protrude from the tips. The sticky-hairy twigs of false azalea are skunky when crushed. The thin, dull, pale green, glandular-hairy leaves are mostly clustered near branch tips and turn crimson in fall. **Where found:** moist woods in foothills and montane zones; from B.C. and Alberta to Wyoming.

Prince's-pine
Chimaphila umbellata

HEIGHT: 4–12 in (10–30 cm)
LEAF LENGTH: ¾–3 in (2–8 cm)
FLOWER WIDTH: less than ½ in (1 cm)
FRUIT WIDTH: ¼ in (5–7 mm)

Prince's-pine has been used to flavor candy, soft drinks (especially root beer), and traditional beers. Native peoples used the tea as a remedy for fluid retention, kidney, or bladder problems, fevers, and coughs. Several native groups smoked the dried leaves. These attractive plants need certain soil fungi to live, so they often die when transplanted. They are best enjoyed in the wild. The leaves of this semi-woody, evergreen shrub are dark, glossy green above and pale beneath. The flowers are waxy and the fruits are round capsules. **Where found:** wooded (usually coniferous) foothills and montane zones; from B.C. and Alberta to Colorado. **Also known as:** pipsissewa.

HERBS

Herbs are non-woody plants. They are usually annuals, although some are perennials that grow from a persistent root stock. Those with flowering stems later produce fruit. Various forms of seeds are familiar, such as those of the sunflower, a favored treat, and the dandelion, whose white parachuted seeds are irresistible fun to blow into the wind. Many herbs are used for adding flavor to foods, and for herbal remedies, aromatherapy, and dyes. The many different and unique flowers give us pleasure for their delicate and often breathtaking beauty in color and form. They are the inspiration of artists and poets and are often symbols of romance, or have meanings attached to them through folklore, legend, or superstition. The herbs illustrated here are the first representatives of each group as they appear in this guide.

LILIES
pp. 136–139

ORCHID
p. 140

EVENING PRIMROSE
p. 140

VALERIAN
p. 140

CARROTS
p. 141

BUCKWHEAT
p. 141

MADDER
p. 142

PINKS
p. 142

SAXIFRAGES
p. 143

PURSLANE
p. 144

DOGWOOD
p. 144

ROSES
pp. 144–145

WATERLILY
p. 146

BUTTERCUPS
pp. 146–147

PEAS
pp. 148–149

VIOLETS
p. 150

MINT
p. 150

DOGBANE
p. 151

CAMPANULA
p. 151

WATERLEAF
p. 151

STONECROP
p. 152

FIGWORTS
p. 152

BORAGE
p. 154

FLAX
p. 154

GERANIUM
p. 154

WINTERGREENS
p. 155

HONEYSUCKLE
p. 155

ASTERS
pp. 156–160

Beargrass
Xerophyllum tenax

HEIGHT: 1½–5 ft (50–150 m)
LEAF LENGTH: 8–24 in (20–60 cm)
FLOWER WIDTH: ½ in (1.5 cm)
FRUIT LENGTH: about ¼ in (5–7 mm)

These densely tufted, evergreen perennials flower only once every 3–10 years, but when conditions are right, their tall, white, bottle-brush clusters cover slopes with white and fill the air with their lily-like perfume. Some native groups used the tough, wiry, grass-like leaves to weave hats, baskets, and capes. The fruits are dry, oval, 3-lobed capsules. **Where found:** dry, open, montane to alpine slopes; from southern B.C. and Alberta to Idaho and Montana.

Mountain Death-camas
Zigadenus elegans; Zygadenus elegans

HEIGHT: 6–28 in (15–70 cm)
LEAF WIDTH: ⅛–⅝ in (0.2–1.5 cm)
FLOWER WIDTH: ¾ in (2 cm)
FRUIT LENGTH: ⅝–¾ in (1.5–2 cm)

This perennial contains the **poisonous** alkaloid zygadenine, which some people claim is more potent than strychnine. Death-camas has been confused with wild onions, blue camas, white hyacinth, and fritillarias, with disastrous results. When in doubt, spit it out! If ingested, induce vomiting and get medical help. Growing from blackish-scaly bulbs, this plant has foul-smelling flowers, each with 6 dark green, heart-shaped glands near its center. The fruits are erect, 3-lobed capsules. Meadow death-camas (*Z. venenosus; Z. gramineus*) has slightly smaller, ½–⅝ in (1–1.5 cm) flowers with rounded glands. **Where found:** moist, open sites in foothills to alpine zones; throughout the Rockies.

Nodding Onion
Allium cernuum

HEIGHT: 4–12 in (10–50 cm)
LEAF WIDTH: ⅛–¼ in (3–7 mm)
FLOWER WIDTH: ¼ in (6 mm)
FRUIT LENGTH: ⅛ in (4 mm)

Many native groups enjoyed wild onions as a vegetable and as flavoring in other foods. Without displaying their flowers, wild onions are distinguished from their poisonous relative, mountain death-camas (above), by their strong onion smell. Do **not** try the taste test. Bears, ground squirrels, and marmots also enjoy wild onions. The ½–¾ in (1–2 cm) thick bulbs are 3-lobed capsules with netted outer layers. **Where found:** moist to dry, open sites in plains, foothills, and montane zones; from B.C. and Alberta south.

Three-spotted Mariposa-lily
Calochortus apiculatus

HEIGHT: 4–12 in (10–30 cm)
LEAF WIDTH: ¼–⅝ in (0.5–1.5 cm)
FLOWER WIDTH: 1¼–1⅝ in (3–4 cm)
FRUIT LENGTH: 1–1¼ in (2.5–3 cm)

These beautiful mountain wildflowers do not transplant well, but they can be grown from seed. Plants take 3–5 years to bloom. The onion-like bulbs were eaten raw or cooked by many native groups and settlers. Bears and rodents also consume the bulbs, and sheep enjoy the nodding, 3-winged seed pods. **Where found:** dry, open sites in foothills and montane zones; from southeastern B.C. and Alberta to Idaho and Montana.

Western Trillium
Trillium ovatum

HEIGHT: 4–16 in (10–40 cm)
LEAF LENGTH: 2–6 in (5–15 cm)
FLOWER WIDTH: 2½–3½ in (6–9 cm)

This wildflower is one of the first showy blooms to grace the forest each spring. Trillium, from the Latin *tri*, 'three,' refers to its 3 leaves, 3 petals, 3 sepals, and 3 stigmas. Each seed has a small, oil-rich body that attracts ants. The ants carry seeds to their nests, eat the oil-rich part, and discard the rest—thus dispersing and planting new trilliums. The fruits are numerous yellowish-green, berry-like capsules, which are shed in a sticky mass. **Where found:** moist to wet, shady sites in foothills to subalpine zones; from B.C. and southwestern Alberta to Colorado.

Western Wood Lily
Lilium philadelphicum

HEIGHT: 1–2 ft (30–60 cm)
LEAF LENGTH: 2–4 in (5–10 cm)
FLOWER WIDTH: 3 in (8 cm)
FRUIT LENGTH: ¾–1⅝ in (2–4 cm)

The cheerful flowers of this leafy perennial brighten woods and roadsides. Unfortunately, digging, mowing, and picking have led to near extinction in many populated areas. The flowers, bulbs, and cylindrical capsules were all eaten by native peoples. The bitter, peppery, whitish bulbs were cooked and mixed with other foods, and they were used in medicinal teas. Tiger lily (*L. columbianum*) has showy clusters of hanging, smaller (1¼–1½ in [3–4 cm]) orange blooms with purple spots. **Where found:** moist, open, or wooded sites in plains, foothills, and montane zones; from B.C. and Alberta south.

Yellow Glacier-lily
Erythronium grandiflorum

HEIGHT: 4–16 in (10–40 cm)
LEAF LENGTH: 4–8 in (10–20 cm)
FLOWER WIDTH: 1¼–2½ in (3–6 cm)
FRUIT LENGTH: 1¼–1⅝ in (3–4 cm)

These lilies blanket mountain slopes soon after snow-melt. The corm-like bulbs of this perennial were eaten raw, but drying and/or cooking made them sweeter and more digestible. Eating too many could cause vomiting. Dried bulbs were a popular trade item among native groups. The leaves and green, 3-sided capsules are said to be edible (cooked), but most native groups used only the bulbs. **Where found:** moist, rich sites in montane to alpine zones; from B.C. and Alberta to Colorado and Utah.

Corn-lily
Clintonia uniflora

HEIGHT: 2½–6 in (6–15 cm)
LEAF WIDTH: 1¼–2 in (3–5 cm)
FLOWER WIDTH: ¾–1 in (2–2.5 cm)
FRUIT WIDTH: ⅜–½ in (0.8–1 cm)

This common woodland wildflower brightens the forest floor in spring and early summer. This sparsely long-hairy perennial has 2–4 slightly fleshy, glossy basal leaves. Although the bright metallic-blue berries are unpalatable by human standards, grouse seem to enjoy them. The species name *uniflora* means 'one-flowered.' **Where found:** moist to wet, montane and subalpine forests and clearings; from B.C. and Alberta to Idaho and Montana. **Also known as:** queen's cup.

Star-flowered False Solomon's-seal
Maianthemum stellatum; Smilacina stellata

HEIGHT: ½–2 ft (15–60 cm)
LEAF LENGTH: 1¼–4¾ in (3–12 cm)
FLOWER WIDTH: less than ½ in (1 cm)
FRUIT WIDTH: ¼–½ in (0.6–1 cm)

The species name *stellata*, from the Latin stella, 'star,' aptly describes the radiant, white flowers of this woodland wildflower. The unbranched, slightly arching plants produce clusters of dark blue or reddish-black berries, which are greenish-yellow with purplish stripes when young. A larger relative, false Solomon's-seal (*M. racemosum*; *S. racemosa*) is easily recognized by its 2–6 in (5–15 cm) long, puffy, pyramidal flower clusters and its wavy (rather than straight-edged) leaves. **Where found:** moist to dry sites in foothills to subalpine zones; from northern Canada to Colorado.

Rough-fruited Fairybells
Disporum trachycarpum

HEIGHT: 1–2 ft (30–60 cm)
LEAF LENGTH: 1¼–3½ in (3–9 cm)
FLOWER LENGTH: ½–⅝ in (1–1.5 cm)
FRUIT WIDTH: about ⅜ in (0.8–1 cm)

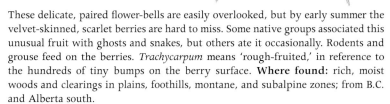

These delicate, paired flower-bells are easily overlooked, but by early summer the velvet-skinned, scarlet berries are hard to miss. Some native groups associated this unusual fruit with ghosts and snakes, but others ate it occasionally. Rodents and grouse feed on the berries. *Trachycarpum* means 'rough-fruited,' in reference to the hundreds of tiny bumps on the berry surface. **Where found:** rich, moist woods and clearings in plains, foothills, montane, and subalpine zones; from B.C. and Alberta south.

Clasping-leaved Twisted-stalk
Streptopus amplexifolius

HEIGHT: 1–3½ ft (30–100 cm)
LEAF LENGTH: 2–6 in (5–15 cm)
FLOWER LENGTH: ⅜–½ in (0.8–1.2 cm)
FRUIT LENGTH: less than ½ in (1 cm)

Hidden beneath the long leaves, these delicate 'bells' and bright red to purple berries are easily overlooked. Some native groups ate the young plants and berries, but immature plants can resemble green false-hellebore shoots (below), which are extremely **poisonous**. *Streptopus*, from the Greek *streptos*, 'twisted,' and *podos*, 'foot,' refers to the bent flower/berry stalks. **Where found:** moist, rich, foothills to subalpine forests and thickets; from northern Canada south.

Green False-hellebore
Veratrum viride; V. eschscholtzii

HEIGHT: 2½–6½ ft (70–200 cm)
LEAF LENGTH: 4–9¾ in (10–25 cm)
FLOWER WIDTH: ¾ in (2 cm)
FRUIT LENGTH: ¾–1¼ in (2–3 cm)

The lush, accordion-pleated leaves of green false-hellebore appear soon after snow-melt. By mid-summer, waist-high plants produce hundreds of musky-smelling flowers in nodding, 12–28 in (30–70 cm) long tassels. The fruits are brown, ovoid capsules. All parts are deadly **poisonous**. Dried plants have been used as a garden insecticide, and water from boiled roots was used to kill lice. **Where found:** moist to wet, open sites in montane to subalpine zones; from northern Canada to Idaho and Montana.

Western Rattlesnake-plantain

Goodyera oblongifolia

HEIGHT: 4–16 in (10–40 cm)
LEAF LENGTH: 1¼–3 in (3–8 cm)
FLOWER LENGTH: ⅝–¾ in (1.5–2 cm)
FRUIT LENGTH: less than ½ in (1 cm)

Some settlers believed that these leaves, with their white, scale-like markings, cured rattlesnake bites—hence rattlesnake-plantain. Children made tiny balloons from the leaves. The downy flowers of this evergreen perennial grow in slender, spiraled, or one-sided clusters. Rein-orchids have similar small, white flowers, but each has a little spur. Also rein-orchid leaves are not white-mottled. **Where found:** dry to moist, shady foothills to montane forests; from B.C. and Alberta south.

Fireweed

Epilobium angustifolium

HEIGHT: 1–10 ft (30–300 cm)
LEAF LENGTH: ¾–8 in (2–20 cm)
FLOWER WIDTH: ¾–1⅝ in (2–4 cm)
FRUIT LENGTH: 1⅝–3 in (4–8 cm)

Fireweed helps heal landscape scars (e.g., roadsides, burned forests) by blanketing the ground with colonies of plants, often producing a sea of deep pink flowers. Young shoots were eaten like asparagus, and the flowers were added to salads. The erect, linear pods split lengthwise to release hundreds of tiny seeds tipped with fluffy, white hairs. Broad-leaved willow-herb (*E. latifolium*) is 6–24 in (15–60 cm) tall, with bluish-green leaves, and 1–7 large, 1¼–2½ in (3–6 cm) wide, purplish-pink flowers. **Where found:** open, often disturbed sites in foothills to subalpine zones; throughout the Rockies.

Sitka Valerian

Valeriana sitchensis

HEIGHT: 1–3½ ft (30–100 cm)
FLOWER WIDTH: ⅛ in (4 mm)
FRUIT LENGTH: ⅛–¼ in (3–6 mm)

If these delicate, pinkish to white flower clusters don't catch your attention, the odor may. Dried, frozen, or bruised plants have a strong, unpleasant smell. The stems are 4-sided and the ribbed, seed-like fruits are tipped with feathery hairs. This perennial was widely used as a sedative. The tranquilizer and muscle relaxant diazepam (Valium) was first extracted from valerian. Marsh valerian (*V. dioica*) is shorter, 4–16 in (10–40 cm), with less than ⅛ in (1–3 mm) flowers and more numerous (9–15) leaflets. **Where found:** moist to wet sites in foothills to subalpine zones; from northern Canada to Idaho and Montana.

Cow-parsnip
Heracleum maximum; H. lanatum

HEIGHT: 3½–8¼ ft (1–2.5 m)
LEAF WIDTH: 4–12 in (10–30 cm)
FRUIT LENGTH: ¼–½ in (0.7–1.2 cm)

Young, fleshy stems of cow-parsnip can be peeled and eaten raw or cooked, but do not confuse cow-parsnip with the **deadly poisonous** water-hemlocks. Many people are sensitive to the hairy skin, and flutes or whistles made from dry, hollow stems may irritate the lips. Many animals, including bears, eat cow-parsnip. This coarse perennial has large leaves, and flattened, egg-to-heart-shaped, broadly winged, ribbed fruits. **Where found:** moist sites in plains to subalpine zones; throughout the Rockies.

White Angelica
Angelica arguta

HEIGHT: 1½–6½ ft (50–200 cm)
LEAFLET LENGTH: 1⅝–4 in (4–10 cm)
FRUIT LENGTH: ⅛–¼ in (4–6 mm)

Although angelicas have been used in herbal remedies, candies, and liqueurs in Eurasia, Rocky Mountain species were not commonly used. White angelica is not poisonous, but it is easily confused with its deadly relatives, the water hemlocks. This robust perennial produces dry, flattened fruits with 2 broad wings. Angelica was taken from the Latin for 'angel,' because the healing powers of the plant were said to be revealed by an angel. **Where found:** moist to wet sites in montane and subalpine zones; from B.C. and Alberta to Utah and Wyoming.

Sulphur Buckwheat
Eriogonum umbellatum; E. subalpinum

HEIGHT: 2–16 in (5–40 cm)
LEAF LENGTH: ½–1¼ in (1–3 cm)
FLOWER WIDTH: less than ⅛ in (2–3 mm)

Of the many buckwheats in the Rocky Mountains, this species is one of the most variable. It can be propagated from seed in dry, sunny rock gardens, but the plants are often difficult to grow. Chipmunks and white-footed mice feast on the seeds, and wild and domestic sheep graze on the plants. This mat-forming perennial has gray-wooly leaves (at least beneath), which become bright red in autumn. The flowers are yellowish, often pinkish-tinged, and the seed-like fruits are smooth and 3-sided seeds. **Where found:** dry, often rocky sites in plains to alpine zones; from B.C. and Alberta to Colorado.

Northern Bedstraw
Galium boreale

HEIGHT: 8–24 in (20–60 cm)
LEAF LENGTH: ¾–2½ in (2–6 cm)
FLOWER WIDTH: ⅛–¼ in (4–7 mm)
FRUIT LENGTH: less than ⅛ in (1.5–2 mm)

Bedstraws are related to coffee, and their tiny, paired, short-hairy nutlets can be dried, roasted, and ground as a coffee substitute. Bedstraw juice or tea was applied to many skin problems. Some people take the tea to speed weight loss, but continual use irritates the mouth, and people with poor circulation or diabetes should not use it. The flowers are in repeatedly 3-forked clusters. Sweet-scented bedstraw (*G. triflorum*) has whorls of 6 broader, bristle-tipped leaves and its nutlets are covered with long, hooked bristles. **Where found:** open sites in foothills and montane zones; throughout the Rockies.

Moss Campion
Silene acaulis

HEIGHT: 1¼–2½ in (3–6 cm)
LEAF LENGTH: ¼–½ in (0.5–1 cm)
FLOWER WIDTH: ¼–⅜ in (6–8 mm)

Dense cushions of 'moss' dotted with bright pink flowers characterize this tiny alpine wildflower. The stiff, withered leaves often persist for many years, and cushions may be 10 years old before they flower. The fruits are erect 3-chambered capsules. Purple mountain saxifrage (*Saxifraga oppositifolia*) is similar, but has tiny, scale-like leaves in 4 vertical rows, and its rose-purple flowers produce clusters of 6–8 spreading pods. **Where found:** moist to well-drained, rocky slopes in subalpine and alpine zones; throughout the Rockies.

Field Chickweed
Cerastium arvense

HEIGHT: 2–12 in (5–30 cm)
LEAF LENGTH: ½–1¼ in (1–3 cm)
FLOWER WIDTH: ⅛–½ in (0.5–1 cm)
FRUIT LENGTH: 2–3½ in (5–9 cm)

These open, flat-topped clusters of cheerful flowers brighten stony slopes. Aptly named, chickweed was fed to chickens, goslings, and caged birds, especially when the birds were ill. The genus name *Cerastium* comes from the Greek *kerastes,* 'horned,' in reference to the curved, cylindrical capsules (which open by 10 small teeth at tip). The leaves of this loosely clumped perennial often have secondary, leafy tufts in their axils. **Where found:** dry, open, often rocky sites in plains to alpine zones; from the Yukon south.

Cut-leaved Foamflower
Tiarella trifoliata; T. unifoliata

HEIGHT: 6–16 in (15–40 cm)
LEAF WIDTH: 1⅝–4 in (4–10 cm)
FLOWER WIDTH: less than ¼ in (5 mm)
FRUIT LENGTH: ⅜–½ in (0.9–1.2 cm)

These delicate, frothy flower clusters grace shady forest floors in mid-summer. Another popular common name, sugar-scoops, refers to the 2 scoop-like parts of each capsule. A related plant, round-leaved alumroot (*Heuchera cylindrica*), has rounded, 5–7-lobed leaves and dense, spike-like flower clusters. It grows on rocky sites in montane to alpine slopes. **Where found:** moist, shaded sites in montane and subalpine zones; from B.C. and Alberta to Idaho and Montana. **Also known as:** sugarscoops.

Spotted Saxifrage
Saxifraga bronchialis

HEIGHT: 2–6 in (5–15 cm)
LEAF LENGTH: ¼–⅝ in (0.5–1.5 cm)
FLOWER WIDTH: ½–⅝ in (0.1–1.5 cm)
FRUIT LENGTH: ⅛ in (4 mm)

These dense prickly, evergreen mats and cushions are an excellent addition to rock gardens. The delicate white flowers are usually dotted with purple, orange, and/or yellow and form small, open clusters. Spotted saxifrage has 2-beaked capsules. *Saxifraga* comes from the Latin *saxum*, 'rock,' and *fragere*, 'to break,' because these plants were thought to break apart the rocks on which they grew. They were also believed to disintegrate gall stones. **Where found:** dry, open, gravelly or rocky sites in foothills to alpine zones; throughout the Rockies.

Fringed Grass-of-Parnassus
Parnassia fimbriata

HEIGHT: 4–12 in (10–30 cm)
LEAF WIDTH: ¾–1⅝ in (2–4 cm)
FLOWER WIDTH: ¾ in (2 cm)
FRUIT LENGTH: less than ½ in (1 cm)

The 5 distinctively fringed, pale-veined petals of these delicate flowers are unmistakable—hence the name *fimbriata*, which means 'fringed.' Each flower has 5 fertile stamens and 5 sterile stamens tipped with 5–9 glands and the fruits are capsules. *Parnassia* comes from Parnassus, a Greek island sacred to Apollo and the muses. Northern grass-of-Parnassus (*P. palustris*) is similar and widespread, but it has smooth-edged petals and its large sterile stamens are tipped with 7–15 glands. **Where found:** wet sites in montane, subalpine, and alpine zones; from northern Canada south.

143

Western Springbeauty

Claytonia lanceolata

HEIGHT: 2–4 in (5–10 cm)
LEAF LENGTH: ⅝–2½ in (1.5–6 cm)
FLOWER WIDTH: ½–⅝ in (1–1.5 cm)
FRUIT LENGTH: ⅛ in (4 mm)

These delicate, fleshy perennials are often found hugging the ground near late snow patches at high elevations. Their leaves are edible, and the corms are said to taste like mild radishes when raw and like potatoes when cooked. Native peoples collected the deep, less than ½ in (1 cm) wide, corms in spring, as the small, white to pinkish blossoms faded. The fruits are egg-shaped capsules. **Where found:** moist, open sites in foothills to alpine zones; from B.C. and Alberta south.

Bunchberry

Cornus canadensis

HEIGHT: 2–8 in (5–20 cm)
LEAF LENGTH: ¾–3 in (2–8 cm)
FRUIT WIDTH: ¼–⅜ in (6–8 mm)

These small flowers are really miniature bouquets of tiny blooms surrounded by showy, petal-like bracts. The true flowers, at the center, are easily overlooked. The large, white bracts attract insects, and provide good landing platforms. The berry-like drupes are edible, raw or cooked. They are not very flavorful, but the crunchy, poppy-like seeds are enjoyable. **Where found:** dry to moist sites in foothills and montane zones; throughout the Rockies.

White Mountain-avens

Dryas octopetala; D. hookeriana

HEIGHT: 4 in (10 cm)
LEAF LENGTH: ¼–1 in (0.5–2.5 cm)
FLOWER WIDTH: ¾–1¼ in (2–3 cm)
FRUIT LENGTH: less than ⅛ in (3 mm)

This alpine wildflower stays low, avoiding cold, drying winds in summer and blanketed by snow in winter. Thick, wrinkled above, and densely white-hairy beneath, these ever-green leaves conserve water and produce food when temperatures rise above freezing. The parabolic flowers follow the sun, warming stigmas and developing seeds. Mature seeds form fluffy heads of ¾–1¼ in (2–3 cm) feathery styles. Another common species, yellow mountain-avens (*D. drummondii*), has nodding, yellow flowers and tapered leaf bases. **Where found:** gravelly sites in subalpine to alpine zones; from Colorado north.

Wild Strawberry

Fragaria virginiana

HEIGHT: 2–6 in (5–15 cm)
LEAF WIDTH: 2–4 in (5–10 cm)
FLOWER WIDTH: ½–¾ in (1.5–2 cm)
FRUIT WIDTH: less than ½ in (1 cm)

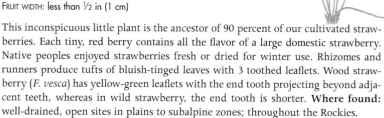

This inconspicuous little plant is the ancestor of 90 percent of our cultivated strawberries. Each tiny, red berry contains all the flavor of a large domestic strawberry. Native peoples enjoyed strawberries fresh or dried for winter use. Rhizomes and runners produce tufts of bluish-tinged leaves with 3 toothed leaflets. Wood strawberry (*F. vesca*) has yellow-green leaflets with the end tooth projecting beyond adjacent teeth, whereas in wild strawberry, the end tooth is shorter. **Where found:** well-drained, open sites in plains to subalpine zones; throughout the Rockies.

Diverse-leaved Cinquefoil

Potentilla diversifolia

HEIGHT: 4–16 in (10–40 cm)
LEAFLET LENGTH: ½–1¼ in (1–3 cm)
FLOWER WIDTH: ⅝–¾ in (1.5–2 cm)

The name *Potentilla* was taken from the Latin *potens*, 'potent,' because these plants stopped bleeding and dysentery in both man and beast. Cinquefoils might be confused with buttercups (*Ranunculus* spp.), but cinquefoil flowers have smaller lobes (bracteoles) alternating with their sepals; these are never found in buttercups. The flowers of this slender perennial produce dense clusters of seed-like fruits protected by the sepals. Graceful cinquefoil (*P. gracilis*) is larger (12–28 in [30–70 cm] tall), and its leaflets are toothed to the base. **Where found:** moist, open sites in foothills to alpine zones; from northern Canada south.

Old Man's Whiskers

Geum triflorum

HEIGHT: 4–12 in (10–30 cm)
LEAF LENGTH: 2–8 in (5–20 cm)
FLOWER WIDTH: ½–¾ in (1–2 cm)
FRUIT LENGTH: less than ⅛ in (3 mm)

At first glance, a field of these plants in seed appears to be covered with low-lying haze—hence 'prairie smoke.' This soft-hairy perennial has 3-flowered clusters of purplish to dusty-pink flowers. Each seed-like fruit has a ¾–1⅝ in (2–4 cm) long, feathery style that carries the fruit on the wind. Native peoples boiled the roots to make a drink flavored like weak sassafras tea. Large-leaved avens (*G. macrophyllum)* has yellow, buttercup–like flowers, and broad, rounded tip leaflets. **Where found:** dry to moist, open sites in plains to subalpine zones; from B.C. and Alberta south. **Also known as:** prairie smoke.

Rocky Mountain Cow-lily
Nuphar lutea; N. polysepalum; N. variegatum

STALK LENGTH: 6½ ft (2 m)
FLOWER WIDTH: 2½–4 in (6–10 cm)
FRUIT LENGTH: 2–3½ in (5–9 cm)

These broad, leathery lily-pads and waxy, yellow flowers are a common sight on quiet waters. Stiff stalks hold the solitary flowers or ribbed capsules at or above the water surface. The huge buried stems have been likened to prehistoric serpents, twisting through the murky depths. Native women collected this starchy food with their toes or dove down in deep water to bring up long chunks. The seeds were also eaten either roasted or ground into flour. **Where found:** shallow ponds and quiet streams in plains to subalpine zones; from Alaska to Colorado.

Cut-leaved Anemone
Anemone multifida

HEIGHT: 6–20 in (15–50 cm)
LEAF WIDTH: 1¼–4¾ in (3–12 cm)
FLOWER WIDTH: ⅝–¾ in (1.5–2 cm)

Anemone leaves contain a strongly irritating, volatile oil, and they were boiled to make a strong tea for killing fleas and lice. Smoke from slowly burning, ripe seed-heads was inhaled to relieve headaches. These plants have little forage value, but they are occasionally eaten by deer and elk. This grayish, hairy perennial has long-stalked flowers with 5–6 creamy white to pink, petal-like sepals that are often reddish or bluish on the outer surface. The silky-wooly, seed-like fruits form dense heads. **Where found:** dry, open sites in foothills, montane, and subalpine zones; throughout the Rockies.

Yellow Columbine
Aquilegia flavescens

HEIGHT: 8–28 in (20–70 cm)
LEAFLET LENGTH: ¾–2 in (2–5 cm)
FLOWER WIDTH: 2 in (5 cm)

These beautiful mountain wildflowers attract long-tongued pollinators (hummingbirds, butterflies), which can reach nectar at the spur tips. Columbine came from the Latin *columbina*, 'dove-like,' because the 5 spreading, petal-like sepals and arched spurs were thought to resemble a circle of 5 doves drinking from a central dish. The fruits of this bluish-green perennial are erect, ¾ in (2 cm) long clusters of 5 pods with spreading tips. Red columbine (*A. formosa*) has red sepals and straight spurs. **Where found:** moist, open sites in foothills to alpine zones; from B.C. and Alberta to Utah and Colorado.

Western Meadowrue
Thalictrum occidentale

HEIGHT: 1–3½ ft (30–100 cm)
LEAFLET LENGTH: ½–1¼ in (1–3 cm)
FRUIT LENGTH: ⅛–⅜ in (5–8 mm)

These tall, delicate woodland plants produce inconspicuous, greenish to purplish, male or female flowers without
petals. The flowers have ⅛–½ in (2–5 mm) long sepals and
either dangling anthers or greenish to purplish, lance-shaped
seeds (achenes), in loose clusters. The pleasant-smelling plants
and seeds were burned in smudges or stored with possessions as
insect repellent and perfume. Chewed seeds were rubbed onto hair and skin as
perfume. Veiny meadowrue (*T. venulosum*) has raised veins on its lower leaf surfaces, and its seeds are broader and smaller (½ in [3–4 mm] long). **Where found:**
moist sites in foothills, montane, and subalpine zones; from B.C. and Alberta to
Colorado.

Baneberry
Actaea rubra

HEIGHT: 1–3½ ft (30–100 cm)
FRUIT LENGTH: about ¼ in (6–8 mm)

Although birds and small mammals eat these tempting,
glossy, red or white berries, baneberry is **toxic** to humans. As
few as 2 berries can cause cramps, headaches, vomiting, bloody
diarrhea, and/or dizziness. Some native peoples considered baneberry
to be sacred and used it in religious ceremonies, but it was always treated
with respect, because it could kill the user. This perennial has long-stalked,
rounded clusters of white flowers each with 5–10 tiny, slender petals. **Where
found:** moist, often shady sites in foothills, montane, and subalpine zones; from
northern Canada south.

Blue Virgin's Bower
Clematis occidentalis; C. verticillaris

HEIGHT: 1½–16 ft (50 cm–500 m)
LEAFLET LENGTH: 1¼–2½ in (3–6 cm)

With its eye-catching blue to purplish flowers and large, fluffy
seed-heads, this woody-stemmed vine makes an excellent ornamental. Propagated
from seed or by layering sections of vine, it grows best in sunny spots where the plant
base is shaded. Each nodding, solitary flower has 4 spreading, 1⅝–2½ in (4–6 cm)
long, petal-like sepals. A common roadside species, white virgin's bower (*C. ligustici-
folia*), has clusters of small, cream-colored flowers. **Where found:** moist to dry, open
sites in foothills and montane zones; from B.C. and Alberta to Utah and Colorado.

Silky Lupine
Lupinus sericeus

HEIGHT: 8–28 in (20–70 cm)
LEAF LENGTH: 1¼–2½ in (3–6 cm)
FLOWER LENGTH: less than ½ in (1 cm)
FRUIT LENGTH: ¾–1¼ in (2–3 cm)

These attractive perennials, with their showy flower clusters and fuzzy seed pods, enrich the soil with nitrogen. Their seed pods look like hairy garden peas, and children may incorrectly assume that they are edible. Many lupines contain **poisonous** alkaloids, and it is difficult to distinguish between poisonous and non-poisonous species. The leaves are silvery-hairy; the pea-like flowers have silky upper sides and form loose, 4–6 in (10–15 cm) long clusters; and the pods have 3–6 seeds. **Where found:** moderately dry, open sites on plains, foothills and montane slopes; from B.C. and Alberta south.

Showy Locoweed
Oxytropis splendens

HEIGHT: 4–12 in (10–30 cm)
LEAF LENGTH: 2–9¾ in (5–25 cm)
FLOWER LENGTH: ½–⅝ in (1–1.5 cm)
FRUIT LENGTH: ⅜–⅝ in (0.8–1.5 cm)

The showy flower clusters of this tufted, densely silky perennial are indeed splendid. Who would think that they could be dangerous? However, many locoweeds contain locoine, an alkaloid that causes horses, sheep, and cattle to go crazy, or 'loco.' The fruits are densely silky, grooved, egg-shaped pods. Showy locoweed is easily identified by its purplish flowers and whorled (rather than paired) leaflets. Of the yellow-flowered locoweeds, silky locoweed (*O. sericea*) has large, 8 in (20 cm) flowers and mountain locoweed (*O. monticola*) has 10–30 flowers per cluster plus 17–33 leaflets per leaf. **Where found:** well-drained, usually open sites in foothills and montane zones; throughout the Rockies.

Yellow Sweet-vetch
Hedysarum sulphurescens

HEIGHT: 6–28 in (15–70 cm)
LEAFLET LENGTH: ½–1⅝ in (1–4 cm)
FLOWER LENGTH: ⅝–¾ in (1.5–1.8 cm)
FRUIT WIDTH: ¼–⅜ in (6–8 mm)

These dense clusters of 20–100 hanging, pale yellow flowers or 'bumpy' pods are hard to miss. Sweet-vetch pods are unmistakable—they look like flattened strings of beads. Yellow sweet-vetch might be confused with American milk-vetch (*Astragalus americanus*), but the milk-vetch has slightly smaller, ½–⅝ in (1.3–1.5 cm) long flowers and inflated, membranous, egg-shaped pods. **Where found:** open, often moist sites in plains to subalpine zones; from B.C. and Alberta to Wyoming.

Northern Sweet-vetch

Hedysarum boreale; H. mackenzii

HEIGHT: 6–24 in (15–60 cm)
FLOWER LENGTH: ½–¾ in (1–2 cm)

Many native groups used sweet-vetch roots for food. Thick
crispy roots were collected in spring or autumn, and eaten raw,
boiled, baked, or fried. Young roots have a sweet, licorice-like
taste, but cooked roots taste like carrots. Grizzly bears also enjoy
eating them. This perennial has reclining to erect, leafy stems and pea-like flowers. Alpine sweet-vetch (*H. alpinum*) is also common, and is easily distinguished
by the regular, conspicuous (rather than obscure) veins on the lower surface of its
leaflets. **Where found:** open sites in foothills, montane, and subalpine zones;
throughout the Rockies.

Alpine Milk-vetch

Astragalus alpinus

HEIGHT: usually less than 4 in (10 cm)
LEAF LENGTH: 1⅝–6 in (4–15 cm)
FLOWER LENGTH: ¼–½ in (0.7–1.2 cm)
FRUIT LENGTH: less than ½ in (1 cm)

These mats of delicate leaves, dotted with short, ½–1⅝ in
(1–4 cm) long clusters of nodding, pale blue or pinkish-purple, pea-like flowers are
common on open gravel flats. Their papery, black-hairy pods do not split open.
Instead, they are blown away by the wind, and are eventually torn apart. Alpine
milk-vetch provides good forage for many animals. Timber milk-vetch (*A. miser*) is
a common tufted species with slender, pointed leaflets and larger ¾–1 in (2–2.5 cm),
hairless or white-hairy pods. **Where found:** open, well-drained sites in montane to
alpine zones; from Colorado north.

Wild Vetch

Vicia americana

HEIGHT: 8–47 in (20–120 cm)
LEAFLET LENGTH: ⅝–1⅜ in (1.5–3.5 cm)
FLOWER LENGTH: 6–8 in (1.5–2 cm)
FRUIT LENGTH: ¾–1¼ in (2–3 cm)

Twining tendrils wrap around nearby stems and leaves as this
slender vine climbs upwards over its neighbors. Its flat, hairless 'pea pods' are
attractive to young children, but they are not edible. When an insect lands on a
vetch flower, anthers spring out to dust its belly with pollen. The next flower collects the pollen on its stigma and applies another load of pollen. **Where found:**
moist, fairly open sites in plains, foothills, and montane zones; from the southern
NWT south.

Early Blue Violet
Viola adunca

HEIGHT: 2–4 in (5–10 cm)
LEAF LENGTH: ½–1¼ in (1–3 cm)
FLOWER WIDTH: about ½ in (1–1.5 cm)
FRUIT LENGTH: ⅛ in (4 mm)

Few of these dainty, blue to violet flowers are fertilized each spring. When no seed is produced, small, inconspicuous blooms appear in autumn, hidden away among debris near ground level. These never open. Instead, they fertilize themselves, producing abundant, fast-growing seeds. Canada violet (*V. canadensis*) has 4–16 in (10–40 cm) tall, leafy stems, broad heart-shaped leaves, and pale whitish flowers with fine purple lines. **Where found:** dry to moist sites in foothills, montane, and subalpine zones; from northern Canada to Colorado.

Round-leaved Yellow Violet
Viola orbiculata

HEIGHT: 2–4 in (5–10 cm)
LEAF WIDTH: ¾–1⅝ in (2–4 cm)
FLOWER WIDTH: about ½ in (1–1.5 cm)

Mature violet capsules shoot their seeds several inches away. Each seed has an oily body (elaiosome) that attracts ants. These industrious insects carry the seeds to their nests, eat the elaiosome, and discard the rest, thus dispersing and planting new violets. All violet plants and flowers are edible, but their roots and fruits are toxic. This leaves of this perennial often lie on the ground and its flowers have fine purple lines. Yellow montane violet (*V. nuttallii*) has tapered leaves that are much longer than wide. **Where found:** moist, wooded sites in foothills and montane zones; in B.C., Alberta, Idaho, and Montana.

Wild Bergamot
Monarda fistulosa

HEIGHT: 8–28 in (20–70 cm)
LEAF LENGTH: 1–3 in (2.5–8 cm)
FLOWER LENGTH: ¾–1½ in (2–3.5 cm)

This showy, aromatic perennial is often grown from seed (smooth nutlets) in gardens. Its long, tubular, rose to purplish flowers attract hummingbirds and hawk moths. The plants provide a spice, potherb, and tea (similar to Earl Grey). Native peoples used the tea to treat ailments ranging from colds and indigestion to pneumonia and kidney problems. Dried leaves were burned or sprinkled on items to repel insects. **Where found:** moist to moderately dry, open sites in plains, foothills, and montane zones; from B.C. and Alberta south. **Also known as:** horsemint.

Spreading Dogbane
Apocynum androsaemifolium

HEIGHT: 8–28 in (20–70 cm)
LEAF LENGTH: ¾–4 in (2–10 cm)
FLOWER LENGTH: ⅛–½ in (0.4–1.2 cm)
FRUIT LENGTH: 2–6 in (5–15 cm)

These delicate, innocent-looking flower-bells can be death-traps. Toothed scales on the petals spring inwards when touched, catching the mouthparts of unsuspecting insects. Butterflies and bees may free themselves, but smaller insects remain trapped and die. Native peoples rolled the tough stem fibers into fine thread and plaited strands to make bowstrings, cord, and nets. This perennial has milky sap. Each sweet-scented flower produces a hanging pair of slender pods that split down one side to release tiny seeds with silky parachutes. **Where found:** well-drained, open sites from plains to subalpine zones; throughout the Rockies.

Common Harebell
Campanula rotundifolia

HEIGHT: 4–20 in (10–50 cm)
LEAF LENGTH: ½–2½ in (1–6 cm)
FLOWER LENGTH: ¾ in (2 cm)
FRUIT LENGTH: ¼–⅜ in (5–8 mm)

From open woodland to exposed, rocky slopes, these delicate, nodding bells bob in the breeze on thin, wiry stems. The small openings at the base of the capsules close quickly in damp weather, protecting seeds from excess moisture. On dry, windy days, the capsules swing widely in the breeze, scattering the seeds. **Where found:** moist to dry, open sites from the plains to subalpine zones; from northern Canada south.

Silky Scorpionweed
Phacelia sericea

HEIGHT: 4–16 in (10–40 cm)
FLOWER WIDTH: less than ¼ in (5–6 mm)

Slender, ½–¾ in (1–2 cm) long stamens project from these tiny flowers, giving the spikes a fuzzy appearance. Elk and other large mammals eat silky scorpionweed, but these hairy, unpleasant-smelling plants cause skin **irritations** in some people. Many phacelias are grown from seed as ornamental plants in rock gardens. The coiled branches of the flower cluster can be compared to the tail of a scorpion. The fruits of this perennial herb are pointed capsules. **Where found:** dry, rocky, open sites in montane to alpine zones; from southern B.C. and Alberta to Colorado.

Lance-leaved Stonecrop
Sedum lanceolatum

HEIGHT: 2–6 in (5–20 cm)
LEAF LENGTH: less than ½ in (1 cm)
FLOWER WIDTH: less than ½ in (1 cm)

These small, hardy perennials grace rugged slopes with flashes of bright yellow. Their succulent, green or reddish leaves (sometimes coated with a whitish, waxy powder) and low growth-form help them to survive in dry, rocky sites. Many stonecrops are cultivated in rock gardens or as house plants. Lance-leaved stonecrop has cylindrical leaves and erect capsules, whereas narrow-petalled stonecrop (*S. stenopetalum*) has flattened leaves and star-like clusters of spreading pods. **Where found:** dry, stony, open sites from plains to alpine zones; from the southern Yukon south.

Slender Blue Penstemon
Penstemon procerus

HEIGHT: 2–16 in (5–40 cm)
LEAF LENGTH: 1⅝–3 in (4–8 cm)
FLOWER LENGTH: ¼–½ in (0.6–1.1 cm)
FRUIT LENGTH: ⅛–½ in (4–5 mm)

This clumped perennial with its whorled clusters of small, intense, bluish-purple flowers would make a beautiful addition to a wildflower garden. Yellow penstemon (*P. confertus*) is similar, but has yellow flowers. Penstemons form a complex group of species (225 from North America). Most have showy clusters of blue to purple, 2-lipped, tubular flowers. *Penstemon*, from the Latin *pente*, 'five,' and *stemon*, 'thread,' refers to the 4 slender, fertile stamens and single, often hairy, sterile stamen in each flower. **Where found:** well-drained, open sites in plains to subalpine zones; from the southern Yukon to Colorado.

Yellow Monkey-flower
Mimulus guttatus

HEIGHT: 4–20 in (10–50 cm)
LEAF LENGTH: ½–2 in (1–5 cm)
FLOWER LENGTH: ½–1⅝ in (1–4 cm)
FRUIT LENGTH: ½–¾ in (1–2 cm)

These snap-dragons brighten streamsides and seeps. *Mimulus* is the diminutive form of the Latin *mimus*, a buffoon or actor in a farce or mime. The common name also alludes to the fancied resemblance of these flowers to small, grinning, ape-like faces. This variable, annual/perennial often roots from nodes or sends out stolons. Its flowers produce oblong capsules inside inflated balloons of fused sepals. Pink monkey-flower (*M. lewisii*) has beautiful 1⅝–2 in (4–5 cm) long, rose-red flowers. **Where found:** wet sites in foothills, montane, and subalpine zones; from northern Canada south.

Sickletop Lousewort

Pedicularis racemosa

HEIGHT: 6–20 in (15–50 cm)
LEAF LENGTH: 1¼–3 in (3–8 cm)
FLOWER LENGTH: ½–⅝ in (1.2–1.5 cm)

Both common names for this species describe the downward-curved, sickle-shaped beak of each flower. Coil-beaked lousewort (*P. contorta*) has very similar flowers, but its calyxes have 5 lobes (not 2) and its leaves appear fern-like, with slender, toothed leaflets. The array of unusual flower forms, found among the louseworts, has evolved to accommodate a variety of specific insect pollinators. This perennial has unbranched, clumped stems, white, sometimes pink-tinged flowers, and flattened, curved capsules. **Where found:** dry, open sites in montane to subalpine zones; from B.C. and Alberta south. **Also known as:** parrot's-beak.

Bracted Lousewort

Pedicularis bracteosa

HEIGHT: 8–39 in (20–100 cm)
LEAF LENGTH: 2½–12 in (6–30 cm)
FLOWER LENGTH: ¾ in (2 cm)

These conspicuous perennials, with their finely divided, fern-like leaves and dense, yellow to reddish flower clusters, are often common on mountain slopes. Each flower produces a curved, flattened capsule. The names Lousewort and *Pedicularis* (from the Latin *pediculus*, 'a little louse') reflect the belief that fields with plenty of lousewort produced cattle infested with lice. Such over-grazed pastures probably did support weak, lice-ridden animals. **Where found:** moist, open sites in lower montane to alpine zones; from B.C. and Alberta to Colorado. **Also known as:** fernleaf.

Scarlet Paintbrush

Castilleja miniata

HEIGHT: 8–24 in (20–60 cm)
LEAF LENGTH: 2–2¾ in (5–7 cm)
FLOWER LENGTH: ¾–1¼ in (2–3 cm)

It is usually easy to recognize a paintbrush, but difficult to say which of the 150–200 species you have. *Castilleja* is a confusing genus, with many flower shapes and colors, and its species often hybridize. Paintbrushes join roots with nearby plants to steal nutrients, and many depend on their neighbors for sustenance. Showy, red bracts give these flower clusters their color. The tubular flowers are greenish with a short, broad lower lip and a long, slender upper lip over half as long as the tube. **Where found:** open sites in foothills and montane zones; from B.C. and Alberta south.

Lemonweed
Lithospermum ruderale

HEIGHT: 8–24 in (20–60 cm)
LEAF LENGTH: 1¼–3 in (3–8 cm)
FLOWER WIDTH: less than ½ in (1 cm)
FRUIT LENGTH: ⅛–¼ in (4–6 mm)

The shiny, whitish to brownish, egg-shaped nutlets (grouped in 4s) of this dryland wildflower were sometimes used by native peoples as decorative beads. They resemble tiny pebbles—hence the name *Lithospermum*, from the Greek *lithos*, 'stone,' and *spermum*, 'seed.' Shoshoni women used the root tea as a contraceptive, and lemonweed extracts have eliminated the estrous cycle in laboratory mice. This loosely tufted perennial produces leafy stems tipped with clusters of pale yellow to greenish flowers. **Where found:** warm, dry sites in plains, foothills, and montane zones; from B.C. and Alberta to Colorado. **Also known as:** yellow puccoon.

Western Blue Flax
Linum lewisii; L. perenne

HEIGHT: 4–28 in (10–70 cm)
LEAF LENGTH: ½–¾ in (1–2 cm)
FLOWER WIDTH: ¾–1¼ in (2–3 cm)

These beautiful, delicate, pale to sky-blue blossoms usually open in the morning and fade in the hot sun later that day. Most plants produce 1 flower at a time, with the next bud opening the following morning. The stems contain long, tough fibers (similar to those of cultivated flax), which have been used to make ropes, cords, fishing lines, and nets. The fruits are round capsules on curved stalks. **Where found:** dry, open sites in plains, foothills and montane zones; throughout the Rockies.

Sticky Purple Geranium
Geranium viscosissimum

HEIGHT: 16–35 in (40–90 cm)
LEAF WIDTH: 1¼–4¾ in (3–12 cm)
FRUIT LENGTH: 9¾–13¾ in (25–35 cm)

The purple veins on these showy pink to magenta petals reflect ultra-violet light. Many insects, such as bees, can see these wavelengths and follow the lines to the nectar at the petal base. Geranium comes from the Greek *geranos*, 'a crane,' because the long, slender capsules resemble crane's-bills. Many geraniums are called crane's-bills or stork's-bills. **Where found:** dry to moist, fairly open sites in foothills and montane zones; from B.C. and Alberta to Colorado.

Pink Wintergreen
Pyrola asarifolia

HEIGHT: 4–12 in (10–30 cm)
LEAF LENGTH: ¾–2½ in (2–6 cm)
FLOWER WIDTH: ⅜–½ in (0.8–1.2 cm)

Like many mountain wildflowers, wintergreens grow in intimate association with soil fungi (mycorrhizae). Some species produce all of their food by photosynthesis, but others take their food almost entirely from dead organic matter via mycorrhizae. These fungi are unlikely to be found in a garden environment, making these plants very difficult to transplant. This shade-loving evergreen has shiny, leathery leaves and round capsule fruits with persistent styles. **Where found:** moist, often shady sites in foothills, montane, and subalpine zones; throughout the Rockies.

Greenish-flowered Wintergreen
Pyrola chlorantha; P. virens

HEIGHT: 3–9¾ in (8–25 cm)
LEAF LENGTH: ½–1¼ in (1–3 cm)
FLOWER WIDTH: ¼–½ in (0.8–1.2 cm)

This delicate denizen of the forest floor is easily identified by its nodding, greenish-white bells, and by the relatively long stalks and small-bladed of its dull, leathery leaves. The leaves are high in methyl salicylate, a natural painkiller, and they can be chewed and applied to wounds as a poultice in an emergency. The fruits of this perennial evergreen herb are round capsules with persistent styles. One-sided wintergreen (*Orthilia secunda*) is less conspicuous, with 4–20 small (¼ in [4–6 mm] wide) flowers all nodding to one side. **Where found:** moist to dry, shaded sites in foothills to subalpine zones; from northern Canada south.

Twinflower
Linnaea borealis

HEIGHT: 1¼–4 in (3–10 cm)
LEAF LENGTH: ½–¾ in (1–2 cm)
FLOWER LENGTH: ¼–⅝ in (6–15 mm)
FRUIT LENGTH: less than ⅛ in (1.5–3 mm)

The small, delicate pairs of pink bells are easily overlooked among other plants on the forest floor, but their strong, sweet perfume may draw you to them in the evening. Hooked bristles on the tiny, egg-shaped nutlets catch on fur, feathers, or clothing of passers-by, who then carry these inconspicuous hitchhikers to new locations. This trailing, semi-woody evergreen is an excellent native ground cover in partially shaded sites. **Where found:** moist, open or shaded sites from foothills to subalpine zones; throughout the Rockies.

Subalpine Fleabane

Erigeron peregrinus

HEIGHT: 4–28 in (10–70 cm)
LEAF LENGTH: 1/2–8 in (1–20 cm)
FLOWERHEAD WIDTH: 3/4–2 1/2 in (2–6 cm)

These star-like flowerheads often appear in native basketry patterns. Fleabanes are easily confused with asters. Aster flowerheads usually have overlapping rows of bracts (involucral bracts) with light, parchment-like bases and green tips. Fleabanes usually have 1 row of slender bracts with the same texture and color (not green) throughout. Also, fleabanes generally flower earlier and have narrower, more numerous rays. Subalpine fleabane has glandular involucral bracts and its seed-like fruits are white to tan with hair-like parachutes. **Where found:** moist to wet, open sites in foothills to alpine zones; from the Yukon south.

Showy Aster

Aster conspicuous

HEIGHT: 12–39 in (30–100 cm)
LEAF LENGTH: 2 1/2–6 in (6–15 cm)
FLOWERHEAD WIDTH: 3/4–1 1/4 in (2–3 cm)

Bright bouquets of showy aster grace woods and meadows in autumn, when other wildflowers have faded. In spring, the sandpapery leaves impart a delicate perfume to your fingertips. This coarse, stiffly hairy perennial has rounded to flat-topped clusters of blue to violet flowerheads and produces hairless, seed-like fruits with whitish, hair-like parachutes. The sound of the wind in the stiff, dry leaves led the Okanagan to name this plant 'rattling noise.' **Where found:** moist to dry, usually open sites in foothills and montane zones; from B.C. and Alberta to Wyoming.

Canada Goldenrod

Solidago canadensis

HEIGHT: 1–4 ft (30–120 cm)
LEAF LENGTH: 2–4 in (5–10 cm)
FLOWERHEAD WIDTH: less than 1/4 in (5 mm)

Many people accuse these bold, pyramid-shaped flower clusters of causing hay fever, but the real culprit is probably a less conspicuous plant, such as ragweed, that shares the same habitat. Goldenrod pollen is too heavy to be carried by the wind; instead, it is carried by flying insects. Each seed-like fruit is tipped with parachutes of white hairs. Missouri goldenrod (*S. missouriensis*) is relatively small (8–19 3/4 in [20–50 cm] tall) with hairless leaves and upper stems and toothless, linear upper leaves. **Where found:** moist, open sites in plains, foothills, and montane zones; from B.C. and Alberta south.

Arrow-leaved Groundsel

Senecio triangularis

HEIGHT: 1–5 ft (30–150 cm)
LEAF LENGTH: 1⅝–8 in (4–20 cm)
FLOWERHEAD WIDTH: ¾ in (2 cm)

This lush, often clumped perennial has triangular leaves and flat-topped clusters of star-like flowerheads. Early herbalists believed that groundsel roots would heal wounds caused by iron objects, and that smelling a root freshly dug by a non-metal tool would cure a headache. The hairless, seed-like fruits are tipped with parachutes of white hairs. **Where found:** moist to wet, fairly open sites in foothills to alpine zones but usually at higher elevations; from northern Canada south.

Curly-cup Gumweed

Grindelia squarrosa

HEIGHT: 8–24 in (20–60 cm)
FLOWERHEAD WIDTH: ¾–1¼ in (2–3 cm)

These bushy, aromatic herbs are common on dry roadsides in late summer. The resin-dotted leaves and flat-topped clusters of sticky flowerheads across have sedative, antispasmodic, and expectorant qualities, and they have been used for many years to treat coughing, congestion, asthma, and bronchitis. Each seed-like fruit has 4–5 ribs. **Where found:** dry, open sites on plains and foothills; from B.C. and Alberta south.

Heart-leaved Arnica

Arnica cordifolia

HEIGHT: 4–24 in (10–60 cm)
LEAF LENGTH: 1⅝–4 in (4–10 cm)
FLOWERHEAD WIDTH: 1–2½ in (2.5–6 cm)
FRUIT LENGTH: ¼–⅜ in (6.5–8 mm)

Some native groups used these cheerful, yellow wildflowers in love charms because of their heart-shaped leaves. Rootstocks and flowers were used in washes and poultices for treating bruises, sprains, and swollen feet, but these **poisonous** plants are never applied to broken skin. This single-stemmed perennial produces seed-like fruits with tufts of white, hair-like bristles. Mountain arnica (*A. latifolia*) has broad (but rarely heart-shaped) leaves that are largest near mid-stem, and its fruit is hairless (at least at the base). **Where found:** open woods and slopes in submontane to subalpine zones; from the Yukon south.

Arrow-leaved Balsamroot

Balsamorhiza sagittata

HEIGHT: 8–28 in (20–70 cm)
LEAF LENGTH: 8–12 in (20–30 cm)
FLOWERHEAD WIDTH: 2–4⅜ in (5–11 cm)
FRUIT LENGTH: ¼–⅜ in (7–8 mm)

In spring, these clumps of radiant, wide sunflowers are unmistakable, but the large, velvety-gray leaves identify arrow-leaved balsamroot year-round. Many parts of these plants were used for food. Young leaves and stems were eaten raw or steamed; the tough, woody, aromatic taproots were cooked, dried, and then soaked overnight; and the hairless, seed-like fruits were dried or roasted and then pounded into flour. **Where found:** dry, often stony grasslands and open woods in foothills and montane zones; from B.C. and Alberta to Colorado.

Brown-eyed Susan

Gaillardia aristata

HEIGHT: 8–28 in (20–70 cm)
LEAF LENGTH: 2–8 in (5–20 cm)
FLOWERHEAD WIDTH: 2–4 in (5–10 cm)
FRUIT LENGTH: about ⅛ in (4 mm)

The flamboyant flowers of brown-eyed Susan might be mistaken for garden escapes, and in fact many cultivars have been developed from this beautiful native wildflower. It is hardy and easily grown from seed. Tea from the roots was taken to relieve stomach and intestinal inflammation, reduce hair loss, and soothe sore eyes. This perennial has hairy leaves and stems, and the seed-like fruits are densely hairy, tipped with 6–10 stiff, white bristles. **Where found:** dry, fairly open sites in foothills and montane zones; from B.C. and Alberta to Colorado. **Also known as:** blanketflower.

Pearly Everlasting

Anaphalis margaritacea

HEIGHT: 8–24 in (20–60 cm)
LEAF LENGTH: 1¼–4 in (3–10 cm)

The papery flower clusters of this hardy perennial grace mountain roadsides for many months. They have a pleasant fragrance, and keep their shape and color when dried—excellent for dried flower arrangements. This erect herb has white-wooly leaves (especially beneath). Pussytoes are similar, but have relatively large basal leaves and small (if any) upper stem leaves. **Where found:** open, moist to dry sites in foothills, montane, and subalpine zones; from B.C. and Alberta south.

Yarrow
Achillea millefolium

HEIGHT: 4–31 in (10–80 cm)
LEAF LENGTH: 1¼–4 in (3–10 cm)
FLOWERHEAD WIDTH: less than ¼ in (5 mm)

This hardy, aromatic perennial has served for thousands of years as a fumigant, insecticide, and medicine. The Greek hero Achilles, for whom the genus was named, used it to heal his soldiers' wounds after battle. Yarrow is an attractive ornamental, but beware—its extensive underground stems (rhizomes) can soon invade your garden. The flowerheads are white (sometimes pinkish) and the seed-like fruits are hairless and flattened. **Where found:** dry to moist, open sites from plains to alpine zones; throughout the Rockies.

Racemose Pussytoes
Antennaria racemosa

HEIGHT: 4–16 in (10–40 cm)
LEAF LENGTH: 1¼–2¾ in (3–7 cm)

Low mats of fuzzy leaves with scattered stalks bearing small, fluffy seed-heads characterize many pussytoes. Racemose pussytoes has hairy stems and bracts with colorless, brownish or reddish tips. Sometimes described as daintily useless, pussytoes were once used to treat liver and small intestine problems. A showier species, rosy pussytoes (*A. microphylla*; *A. rosea*), has heads of white to pinkish bracts. **Where found:** dry to moist, wooded or open sites in montane and subalpine slopes; from B.C. and Alberta to Wyoming.

Slender Hawkweed
Hieracium gracile

HEIGHT: ¼–14 in (3–35 cm)
LEAF LENGTH: ½–3 in (1–8 cm)
FLOWERHEAD WIDTH: less than ½ in (1 cm)

Loose clusters of miniature dandelions on long, slender stems mark this common wildflower. These showy flowerheads attract insects, but fertilization is rare. Most offspring are genetically identical to the parent plant. Hawkweed's milky sap contains a rubbery latex, and native peoples chewed the leaves of these plants like gum. The fruits are cylindrical achenes with tufts of tawny hairs. Hound's-tongue hawkweed (*H. cynoglossoides*; *H. albertinum*) has taller (12–40 in [30–100 cm]) stems with large (2–8 in [5–20 cm] long) leaves. **Where found:** moist to wet, open sites from foothills to alpine zones; from northern Canada south.

159

Orange Agoseris
Agoseris aurantiaca

HEIGHT: 4–24 in (10–60 cm)
LEAF LENGTH: 2–14 in (5–35 cm)
FRUIT LENGTH: ¼–⅜ in (5–9 mm)

This attractive mountain wildflower resembles an orange dandelion. Its milky sap contains rubbery compounds, and some native peoples chewed the leaves of these plants like gum. Each smooth, seed-like fruit is tipped with a long, slender beak, bearing a star-burst of white hairs. Short-beaked agoseris (*A. glauca*) has yellow flowerheads and its fruits have short, stout, ribbed beaks. Nodding microseris (*Microseris nutans*) resembles short-beaked agoseris, but its pappus hairs are scale-like at the base and feathery at their tips (not simply hair-like). **Where found:** dry to moist, open sites in foothills to alpine zones; from B.C. and Alberta south.

WEEDS

Many of the most common wildflowers along roads and in fields and towns did not grow here less than 200 years ago. Most of these highly successful plants, or weeds, originated in Europe and Asia. Some arrived accidentally, mixed with other plant products such as seed or hay, but many were brought here purposely as crops, medicinal plants, and garden flowers. Since their arrival, many of the hardier and more aggressive plants have left the garden and cultivated field, and spread to suitable sites across the continent. Most seem to prefer disturbed ground, often associated with human activity, but others are expanding into natural habitats, where they can replace less aggressive native plants. The most successful invaders are classified as noxious weeds, and although many are very pretty, they are troublesome pests in the human setting and a threat to plant communities in the wild.

MEADOW BUTTERCUP
Ranunculus acris

BUTTER-AND-EGGS;
COMMON TOADFLAX
Linaria vulgaris

GREAT MULLEIN;
COMMON MULLEIN
Verbascum thapsus

YELLOW SWEET-CLOVER
Melilotus officinalis

ALFALFA
Medicago sativa

RED CLOVER
Trifolium pratense

ALSIKE CLOVER
Trifolium hybridum

WHITE CLOVER
Trifolium repens

TEASEL
*Dipsacus fullonum;
D. sylvestris*

OXEYE DAISY
*Leucanthemum vulgare;
Chrysanthemum
leucanthemum*

PINEAPPLE WEED
*Matricaria dicoidea;
M. matricarioides*

COMMON TANSY
Tanacetum vulgare

ANNUAL HAWKSBEARD
Crepis tectorum

YELLOW SALSIFY;
GOAT'S-BEARD
Tragpogon dubius

PERENNIAL SOW-THISTLE
*Sonchus arvensis;
S. uliginosus*

COMMON DANDELION
Taraxacum officinale

CHICORY
Cichorium intybus

SPOTTED KNAPWEED
*Centaurea biebersteinii;
C. maculosa*

CANADA THISTLE
Cirsium arvense

BULL THISTLE
Cirsium vulgare

161

CLIMATE

The wide range of elevations and latitudes found in the Rockies results in a highly variable climate. A rise of 100 m in elevation has been equated to traveling over 300 km north (a rise of 1000 ft in elevation has been equated to traveling 600 mi north). Temperatures are generally cool in the mountains, with annual averages ranging from about 36.5° F (2.5° C) in the Canadian Rockies to about 50° F (10° C) in the Southern U.S. Rockies. These cool temperatures are, in large part, because of the cooling associated with higher elevations. The standard temperature change or 'lapse rate' with increasing elevation is about -2.5 to -3.5° F/1000 ft (or -0.5 to -1.0° C for every 100 m of elevation). For this reason, it can easily be 50–59° F (10–15° C) cooler on a mountain peak than in a nearby valley bottom. Subalpine areas may also be cooled by cold, dense air flowing down from glaciers, snow, or frozen ground at higher elevations. Above 9000 ft (2750 m) elevation, freezing temperatures can occur on any night of the year.

Because the atmosphere is thinner at higher elevations, ultraviolet radiation is approximately 25 percent higher at 14,000 ft (4275 m) elevation than it is at 5500 ft (1675 m). Also, at higher elevations, there is less oxygen. Many people experience shortness of breath above 8000 ft (2440 m); air above 10,000 ft (3050 m) has about ⅔ as much oxygen as air at sea level. Some visitors experience 'mountain sickness' or 'elevation sickness' in high areas, often suffering from headaches, nausea, and general fatigue. It is recommended that you allow yourself 2–3 days to acclimate before undertaking strenuous physical activity at high elevations.

The mountain climate also varies dramatically with changes in latitude, as temperatures decline from south to north. The effects of this temperature change can be seen in the gradual lowering of the treeline (the edge of alpine tundra) from south to north. For example, treeline is generally at 10,825–11,810 ft (3300–3600 m) elevation in Colorado, whereas in Alberta it ranges from 6560–7545 ft (2000–2300 m). Treeline is said to shift by approximately 360 ft (110 m) with every degree of latitude.

Prevailing winds blow from west to east across the Rockies, and as the air from the Pacific rises, it cools and drops much of its moisture as rain or snow on the western slopes, leaving the eastern slopes noticeably drier and cooler. The Canadian range of the Rockies lies closest to the Pacific coast, and it receives large amounts of rain and snow as moisture-laden air rises to flow over its peaks. Southern segments of the Rockies are farther from the ocean and are therefore drier. Southern areas also tend to be warmer, and with higher temperatures come increased evaporation, drier soils, smaller rivers, fewer glaciers, and longer growing seasons.

THE SEASONS

Spring, summer, autumn, and winter seasons all affect the lives of plants, animals, and people in the Rockies. Spring is generally short, characterized by warmer weather, mixtures of rain and snow, and the re-emergence of plant life. Millions of birds pass over and along the Rockies on their way to northern breeding grounds, while bears and other hibernating creatures awaken and emerge from their long winter slumber. Glacier lilies and cut-leaved anemones are some of the first wildflowers to bloom, often bursting through the last remnants of snow. Longer days of sunshine bring forth the buds of trees and shrubs, which in turn whet the appetites of browsing mammals and munching insects. Only an uncomfortable encounter with a spring blizzard or intrusive wood tick can put a damper on a beautiful spring day in the Rockies.

Summer is the most popular time of year for tourists. Warmer, longer days of sunshine bring forth wildflower blooms, pupating insect larvae, hawking birds, and newborn animals. Many young animals are born in early summer. Trails, roads, lakes, streams, campgrounds, and townsites suddenly swell with both wildlife and people. Many wonderful, memorable encounters and the occasional conflict between wild animals and tourists mark every summer in the Rockies. Marmots, bats, bears, hummingbirds, warblers, frogs, snakes, fish, insects, and wildflowers are all active under the summer sun. The odd summer snowstorm and swarm of mosquitoes add a dimension of challenge to visiting the mountains. Fortunately, these challenges quickly yield to the spectacular and unforgettable sight of late blooming wildflowers in the high alpine.

Like spring, autumn is brief but unmistakably colorful and alive. Trembling aspen, western larch, and alpine larch brighten mountain forests with intense bursts of yellow. The sounds of crashing horns from sparring bighorn rams and the surreal bugling of male elk echo across mountain slopes and through crisp autumn forests. Deer and moose also keep the rutting activity lively as migrating birds fly south to warmer wintering grounds. In response to shortening daylight hours, many plants quickly drop their leaves and send their nutrients down into roots and tubers to be stored safely until spring. Bears systematically search meadows and forest openings for patches of juicy, fattening, wild berries. Many people consider autumn to be the loveliest of Rocky Mountain seasons.

Bitter, cold winds, large amounts of snow, and the arrival of many anxious skiers announce the onset of winter. Throughout the season there are plenty of tranquil, not so chilly days on which to enjoy the outdoors. Cross-country skiing and snowshoeing are excellent means of traveling through snow-drenched forests to see pine martens, white-tailed ptarmigans, northern hawks, and owls. Many hours of excitement can be had by trying to follow and identify the tracks of secretive animals recorded in the snow. Otter slides and the tracks of cougars, elk, weasels, and red squirrels are easy to find in winter conditions. All animals and plants that remain in the Rockies over winter have special adaptations that allow them to survive in the most brutal winter weather. Many birds and mammals that spend their summers at higher elevations move down to warmer, sheltered valleys for winter. Reptiles, amphibians, most insects, bears, and some smaller mammals hibernate at this time of year, rather than struggle through the cold, foodless winter.

PEOPLE IN THE ROCKIES
Aboriginal Peoples & Pioneers

The Rocky Mountains represent a variety of landscape features, ecological processes, and communities of plants and animals that are scientifically estimated to be billions of years in the making. These features, processes, and communities are continually changing and evolving together as interconnected and inseparable parts of a greater whole that we call the Rockies. The Rockies are, in turn, only a small part of an even greater whole we call the Earth. To truly know these mountains, we attempt to understand not only the plants and animals that live in the Rockies, but also the significance of these creatures and the mountains within a larger global community.

For thousands of years, wildfires, insects, and disease played their small part in shaping the ecology of the Rockies, forcing plants and animals to develop ingenious ways of surviving and thriving. Similarly, aboriginal peoples survived within the community's limitations while simultaneously changing the environment and ecology as they hunted, fished, gathered plants, and built shelters.

People have been a part of nature in the Rocky Mountains for over 10,000 years. Very few of these people lived in the Rocky Mountains year-round; they spent most of the cold, snowy winter months at lower elevations, and traveled up to the mountains during summer to hunt and gather plants. Native peoples in the Rocky Mountains are generally classified as belonging to the Great Basin Region (from northern New Mexico north to central Idaho), the Plateau Region (from central Idaho to just south of Jasper), or the Western Sub-arctic Region (areas north of Jasper).

The history of the many native groups found within each region is complex, unique, and truly important to the evolution of Rocky Mountain nature. The people within each region were forced to find unique solutions to survive under varied climatic and geologic conditions. Plants that were gathered and animals that were hunted or trapped in various seasons provided the people with food, clothing, shelter, and spirituality. The importance of plants varied greatly throughout the Rockies. Trees, for example, provided wood, pitch, bark, and roots; mosses provided absorbent diapers; and many plants provided medicines and food.

More recent historical events have resulted in the tragic loss of much ancestral native knowledge and culture. Fortunately, the study of ethnobotany—the study of the relationships between people and plants—and the revival of native traditions may bring about the return of some of these remarkable, ancient ways.

The late 1700s and early 1800s marked a turning point in human existence in the Rockies. European contact with native peoples brought death and suffering through disease, war, or famine, which was caused by the extermination of the great bison herds. As early as the 1600s, Spaniards moving north from Mexico established the city of Santa Fe and laid claim to lands as far north as Colorado. Later, French, English, and American fur traders moved into the Rockies in search of fur-bearing animals. Explorers in search of a 'Northwest Passage' to the Pacific Ocean crossed the continent in droves. During their historic journeys, they made many of the first scientific observations of western nature and culture.

In the U.S., pioneering fur traders and rugged 'mountain men' often lived among the native peoples and were responsible for finding safe passage for settlers across the previously impenetrable spine of the Rockies. With the establishment of the Oregon Trail through Wyoming and into southeastern Idaho, settlers from the East were able to traverse the Rockies on their way to settle Idaho, Washington, Oregon, California, Nevada, and Utah. In Canada, settlers moved into and through the Rockies mainly through the Yellowhead Pass near Jasper. In the 1880s, the building of the transcontinental Canadian Pacific Railway (CPR) heralded the onset of the Rockies as a tourist mecca for the next hundred years and beyond. CPR president William Van Horne supported the formation of Banff and Yoho national parks through which the railway ran.

Increasingly, humans have become a greater part of the Rocky Mountains, accelerating the processes of change, for better or for worse. Many people argue that the fast rate at which we are transforming the landscape will irrevocably harm the Rockies. Rapid settlement and exploitation of the Rockies through mining, grazing, energy production, and timber extraction has led to the creation of cities, towns, highways, forest reserves, and protected areas. Today, the parks, monuments, and wilderness areas of the Rocky Mountains represent many of the last, best wilderness areas in North America south of the Arctic Circle.

It is the responsibility of those of us who find inspiration and joy in the Rockies to do our part to promote the continued survival of this great wilderness. The Yellowstone to Yukon initiative is one effort that currently seeks to expand the existing network of protected areas. It will link animal corridors and buffer zones, allowing animals free movement. Please help keep the Rockies beautiful to our eyes and wild in our hearts!

Sasquatch

Height: 6–8 ft (1.8–2.4 m)

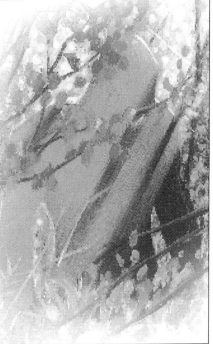

Each year there are reports of huge human-like footprints, larger than a grizzly bear's, imprinted in the soft shores of a mountain stream—or a large, hairy, human/ape-like animal disappearing into the forest. Is it a bizarre-looking bear or wolverine? Or do remnants of an ancient, human/ape-like species roam the Rocky Mountains? Could this nocturnal and nomadic species survive in the mountain environment without leaving proof of its existence? Keep your camera ready! You could be the first to prove the existence of the sasquatch! **Where found:** possibly throughout the Rockies. **Also known as:** bigfoot.

PARKS & PROTECTED AREAS
Alberta

A BANFF NATIONAL PARK (2564 MI²/6640 KM²)

Canada's first national park offers world-renowned scenery and excellent chances to see stunning flora and fauna. Lake Louise, Peyto Lake and Moraine Lake are but a few of the jewels of Banff National Park. The looping alpine meadow trails at Bow Summit are accessible to everyone and provide visitors with good chances to see spring azures, Clark's nutcrackers, rufous hummingbirds, golden eagles, golden-mantled ground squirrels, bighorn sheep, subalpine fir, yellow glacier-lilies, white mountain-avens, and scarlet paintbrushes.

B JASPER NATIONAL PARK (4200 MI²/10,878 KM²)

Grizzly bears, black bears, gray wolves, mountain caribou, elk, mule deer, moose, mountain lions, and bighorn sheep all roam the wilds of this large park. Look for sheep and wolves at the north end of Jasper Lake; caribou, mink, and moose along Medicine River; black swifts in Maligne Canyon; bears along the Icefields Parkway; and wonderful trees, shrubs, and flowers everywhere you look! Visitors can hike on the toe of the 6 mi (10 km) long Athabasca Glacier and learn about geological processes first-hand.

C WATERTON LAKES NATIONAL PARK (203 MI²/526 KM²)

Forming the Canadian part of the Waterton-Glacier International Peace Park, Waterton, located where the prairies meet the mountains, contains a unique mix of grasslands, forests, alpine tundra, and vital aquatic habitats. The variety of habitats results in tremendous species diversity. Wild roses, beargrass, dragonflies, rainbow trout, western long-toed salamanders, bull snakes, white-tailed ptarmigans, Townsend's solitaires, golden eagles, beavers, pikas, mountain goats, and bighorn sheep are all here.

D1 KANANASKIS COUNTRY **D2** PETER LOUGHEED PROVINCIAL PARK (1600 MI²/4100 KM²)

Winter in the front ranges of the Rockies is magical, revealing the tracks of mountain lions, wolves, snowshoe hare, and elk, while tall stands of lodgepole pine clothe themselves in soft pillows of snow. In spring and summer, the forests and mountain slopes echo with the calls of ravens and the sweet songs of blue-headed vireos, rock wrens, yellow-rumped warblers, western tanagers, and white-crowned sparrows. American dippers dive in icy waters for caddisfly larva, and great horned owls scan the flowery forest floor in search of voles and shrews.

E WILLMORE WILDERNESS PARK (1075 MI²/2784 KM²)

This rugged, remote, mountainous park contains many complex and dynamic communities of plants and animals: hummingbirds, butterflies, moths, and other insects pollinate herbaceous wildflowers and flowering shrubs; songbirds snatch insects for food and plant material for nest construction; and mammals feed on plants, insects, birds, fish, or other mammals. Mountain rocks erode, and rains transport broken materials and nutrients into flowing streams for their long journey to the sea.

F CASTLE CROWN WILDERNESS (286 MI/740 KM²)

Bordering the northern boundary of Waterton Lakes National Park, this relatively unknown wilderness is unprotected from human development. The front range mountains and canyons, lush backcountry valleys, clean headwater streams, and jagged peaks of the Continental Divide provide critical habitat for many endangered and threatened plant and animal species, including bull trout, wolves, grizzly bears, and 35 species of plants considered to be rare in Alberta.

G1 WHITE GOAT **G2** SIFFLEUR WILDERNESS AREAS (331 MI²/856 KM²)

These small, front-range rugged wilderness areas protect a wide variety of species and their habitats. Dayhikes or multi-day backcountry trips during summer are sure to reveal mourning cloaks, western toads, blue grouse, a flock of white-winged crossbills, least chipmunks, and some mule deer. Lucky observers may get a good look at an American dipper, brook trout, a pair of harlequin ducks, a drilling pileated woodpecker, gray-crowned rosy-finches, a porcupine, a hoary bat, a marten, or a lynx.

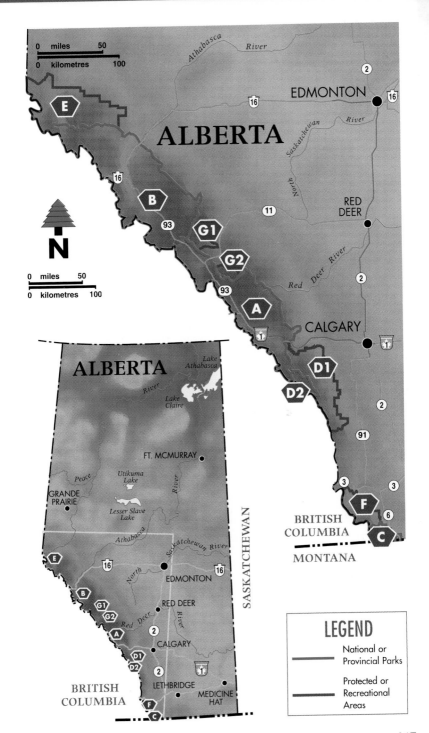

British Columbia

A YOHO NATIONAL PARK (507 MI²/1313 KM²)
The melting Daly Glacier, nestled among the towering peaks of the Continental Divide, gives rise to spectacular Takakkaw Falls, whose water plummets 1248 ft (380 m) into the wild Yoho River. Moose, deer, and elk may be found at the salt lick near the amazing natural bridge. At Emerald Lake, look for lovely wildflower displays along the trailsides and avalanche slopes. Yoho's Burgess Shale World Heritage Site contains the fascinating fossil remains of marine animals estimated to be 530 million years old.

B KOOTENAY NATIONAL PARK (543 MI²/1406 KM²)
Kootenay's ochre-tinted paint pots and myriad wild plants were once used by the Kootenai Nation for ceremonial and survival needs. In more recent times, this magnificent mountain park's natural hot springs and many natural salt licks have made it a special environment.

C GLACIER NATIONAL PARK (521 MI²/1350 KM²)
This awe-inspiring park is like a natural cathedral, with soaring snow-capped peaks and glistening turquoise glaciers. Luxurious alpine meadows full of wildflowers, jagged talus slopes echoing with the high-pitched alarm calls of pikas, and deeply cut valleys channeling raging whitewater rivers support a diversity of life.

D MOUNT REVELSTOKE NATIONAL PARK (100 MI²/260 KM²)
Mt. Revelstoke is one of the few parks that has easy access to the flower-filled alpine meadows of summer. Visitors encounter radiant expanses of flowers along the Sky Trail, with the option of continuing to the jewel-like Eva, Miller, and Jade Lakes. The short Giant Cedars Boardwalk Trail embraces visitors and wildlife in a moist atmosphere of beauty.

E MOUNT ROBSON & REARGUARD FALLS PROVINCIAL PARKS (848 MI²/2196 KM²)
At 12,972 ft (3954 m), Mount Robson is the highest peak in the Canadian Rockies. Berg Glacier, on the north face, occasionally calves massive chunks of ice into Berg Lake. Backcountry trails link hikers to Jasper National Park and typical high-country wildlife, while the marshes of Moose Lake give highway travelers a chance to see moose and many species of waterfowl. At Rearguard Falls, watch for chinook salmon jumping the final barrier to reach their spawning grounds after an 800 mi (1300 km) journey from the Pacific.

F MOUNT ASSINIBOINE PROVINCIAL PARK (150 MI²/388 KM²)
Renowned as Canada's Matterhorn, Mount Assiniboine is only accessible by foot, horse, or in winter months by snowshoe or ski. Adventurous and observant visitors are sure to meet mountain avens, gray-crowned rosy-finches, and bighorn sheep, and to hear the howling of wolves.

G1 WELLS GRAY PROVINCIAL PARK **G2** CARIBOO MOUNTAINS PROVINCIAL PARK
G3 BOWRON LAKE PROVINCIAL PARK (>3000 MI²/ >7800 KM²)
The long, slim lakes of Bowron Lake Provincial Park provide a spectacularly scenic, 73 mi (117 km) canoeing-portaging experience unrivaled in North America. To the south, the Cariboo Mountains and Wells Gray provincial parks are filled with shimmering lakes, streams, and waterfalls, extinct volcanoes, colorful, fragrant plants, and exciting wildlife.

H1 KOKANEE GLACIER PROVINCIAL PARK & RECREATION AREA
H2 VALHALLA PROVINCIAL PARK (>270 MI²/>700 KM²)
These two parks nestled in the Selkirk Mountains of southeastern B.C. are relatively small islands of wildness surrounded by areas allocated for forestry and other development. Kokanee Creek and other tributaries of nearby Kootenay Lake provide spawning habitat for landlocked sockeye salmon (called kokanee, meaning 'red fish').

I BUGABOO GLACIER PROVINCIAL PARK & ALPINE RECREATION AREA (96 MI²/250 KM²)
This specially regulated protected area gives visitors a first-hand experience with nature. Backcountry hiking, mountain climbing, ski-touring, and glacier travel expose trained adventurers to raw elements and rarely seen natural wonders.

J MUSKWA-KECHIKA MANAGEMENT AREA (4245 MI²/10,995 KM²)
In the fall of 1997, the government of British Columbia announced the protection of over 1 million hectares of wilderness in B.C.'s northern Rockies. This celebration of wilderness conservation will afford protection for many large and dynamic communities of wild plants and animals. The creation of this park is a major contribution to the Yellowstone to Yukon initiative, which seeks to connect a series of large protected areas.

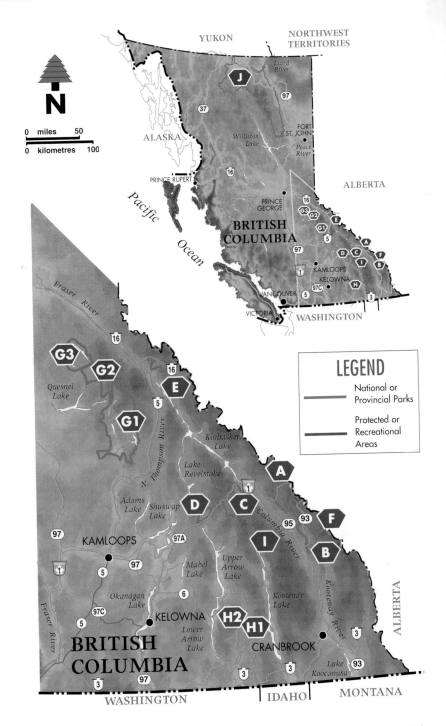

LEGEND

National or Provincial Parks

Protected or Recreational Areas

Montana

A GLACIER NATIONAL PARK (1562 MI²/4045 KM²)

The Going-to-the-Sun Road (closed in winter) is one of Montana's most spectacular drives, with many roadside turnouts from which to enjoy the scenery. Although humans tend to be the most abundant species in summer, mountain goats, bighorn sheep, mule deer, and both species of bear are regularly near roadways. Late summer wildflower blooms and alpine larch in fall colors are spectacular at higher elevations. Lake McDonald and its old-growth shores provide excellent habitat for both aquatic and forest-dwelling species.

B1 GREAT BEAR **B2** BOB MARSHALL **B3** SCAPEGOAT WILDERNESS AREAS (>2350 MI²/>6085 KM²)

Straddling the Continental Divide, these great wilderness areas are administered by the U.S. Forest Service. They are vital links in the chain of mountain wilderness extending south from the Waterton-Glacier International Peace Park. Precipitous, rocky peaks, colorful alpine meadows, and rich forested valleys harbor many interesting wild plants and animals. Forestry roads and state highways provide access to the campgrounds and trailheads on the perimeter of these areas.

C RED ROCK LAKES NATIONAL WILDLIFE REFUGE (63 MI²/163 KM²)

This refuge just west of Yellowstone National Park protects important nesting habitat for trumpeter swans, great blue herons, Barrow's goldeneyes, and sandhill cranes. From mid-July to late autumn, quietly canoeing the refuge's lakes, marshes, and streams is an excellent way to see these birds and other water-dwelling residents, including muskrats, beavers, common yellowthroats, red-winged blackbirds, water shrews, dragonflies, tiger salamanders, and lake chub. Wildlife viewing areas also overlook aquatic and grassland species.

D BITTERROOT WATCHABLE WILDLIFE TRIANGLE (>4 MI²/>11 KM²)

The 60 mi (97 km) long Bitterroot Valley south of Missoula offers a first-hand experience with Rocky Mountain nature. The Charles Waters Nature Trail, the Lee Metcalf National Wildlife Refuge, and the Willoughby Environmental Education Area, all near Stevensville, provide nature trails and wildlife-viewing blinds in excellent wildlife habitat. Ospreys, belted kingfishers, otters, muskrats, herons, frogs, garter snakes, porcupines, deer, interesting insects, and a whole host of songbirds can be observed depending on the season.

E NATIONAL BISON RANGE (30 MI²/75 KM²)

On the Flathead Indian Reservation at the southern end of the Flathead Valley, the legacy of the bison continues, even though these mighty creatures no longer enjoy the numbers and freedom they once had. Elk, mule deer, white-tailed deer, bighorn sheep, and pronghorn share the valley bottom range with up to 500 bison within the confines of perimeter fences. The two-hour Red Sleep Mountain self-guided drive gives a close-up view of bison and the 50 animal species and 200 bird species recorded here. Pablo and Ninepipe National Wildlife Refuges are also on the reservation north of the National Bison Range.

F ANACONDA-PINTLER WILDERNESS (248 MI²/642 KM²)

The 280 mi (451 km) of trails wind through deep U-shaped valleys, over glacial moraines, and around cirque lakes from 5100–10,793 ft (1555–3290 m) elevation. Moose, boreal chorus frogs, bull trout, song sparrows, and willows thrive in the valley bottoms at lower elevations, while mountain goats, cutthroat trout, horned larks, and moss campion dominate the high country. Black bears, grizzly bears, and hoary marmots dream away cold mountain winters, while bobcats, coyotes, and elk leave a record of their travels on snowy ground.

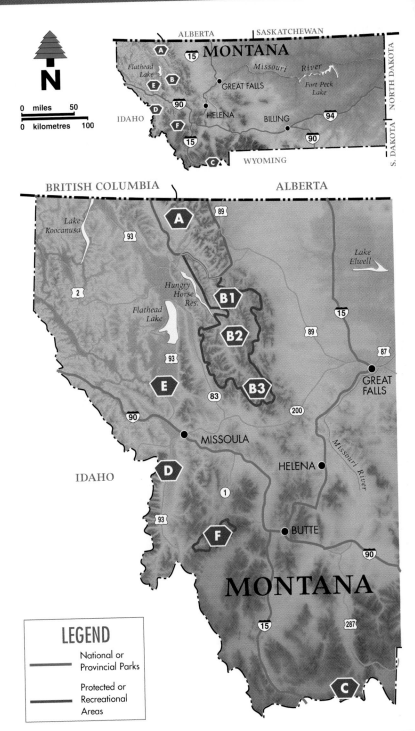

Idaho

A SELWAY-BITTERROOT WILDERNESS AREA (1530 MI²/3950 KM²)

Hundreds of miles of maintained trails give the more intrepid visitors to northeastern Idaho non-motorized access to cool, old-growth Douglas-fir forests, clear mountain streams, flowery meadows, and rocky slopes. Picnic areas and campgrounds are on the perimeter of the wilderness for those unable to make the commitment to backcountry pursuits. Gray jays, least chipmunks, and white-tailed deer add magic to the towering trees and growing plants of both front-country and backcountry campgrounds.

B1 SAWTOOTH NATIONAL RECREATION AREA **B2** SAWTOOTH WILDERNESS AREA **B3** LAND OF THE YANKEE FORK STATE PARK (>1500 MI²/>3900 KM²)

The Sawtooth, Boulder, and White Cloud mountains cradle over 300 alpine lakes and form the headwaters of five major rivers. Lodges, guest ranches, and campgrounds, picnic areas, and dayhike trails allow you to investigate the flora and fauna while taking in the local culture. Backcountry trails, campsites are also available.

C CRATERS OF THE MOON NATIONAL MONUMENT (83 MI²/215 KM²)

Situated at the southern base of Idaho's Pioneer Mountains, this national monument protects an astonishing biotic community in a harsh volcanic, desert environment. Hardened lava tubes, spatter cones, cinder cones, and lava flows (including pahoehoe, aa, and blocky flow types) are some of the incredible volcanic features that may be seen along the monument's 7 mi (1.6 km) self-guided loop drive and many hiking trails. During summer, western rattlesnake, western skink, and short-horned lizard are all here. Snowshoeing, cross-country skiing, animal tracking, and photography are popular winter activities.

D FRANK CHURCH-RIVER OF NO RETURN WILDERNESS (3594 MI²/9308 KM²)

Acclaimed as the largest wilderness area in the lower 48 states, this place of whitewater rivers, thriving natural forest communities, and majestic mountains is especially known for its large population of secretive mountain lions. Marten, fisher, red fox, wolverine, hawks, eagles, falcons, and owls all thrive among healthy prey populations of small mammals, fish, reptiles, and amphibians. Rafting tours and horseback trips combine mountain adventure with nature appreciation.

E GRAYS LAKE NATIONAL WILDLIFE REFUGE (29 MI²/74 KM²)

Established to protect breeding cranes and waterfowl, this lake may produce up to 5000 ducks, 2000 geese, and 150 sandhill cranes in a single breeding season. Attempts are also being undertaken to encourage endangered whooping cranes to nest in this large, shallow wetland. This area boasts sightings of 199 species of birds and up to 3000 sandhill cranes in a single day from late September to early October. A wildlife viewing platform is next to the ranger station, but most of the area is sensitive to human disturbance and is therefore closed to visitors.

F KOOTENAI NATIONAL WILDLIFE REFUGE (4 MI²/11 KM²)

A mix of small wetlands, grasslands, forests, shrublands, and cultivated croplands provide sanctuary for a variety of species and provide good wildlife viewing opportunities. During spring migration, hundreds of tundra swans, mallards, northern pintails, and American wigeons use this area for refueling on their way north, while in fall, over 2000 Canada geese use the area on their way south. From spring to autumn, frogs, turtles, salamanders, snakes, songbirds, raptors, and insects can be seen among the refuge's diversity of trees, shrubs, and flowers.

G BEAR LAKE NATIONAL WILDLIFE REFUGE (27 MI²/71 KM²)

Straddling the Idaho–Utah border, Bear Lake's turquoise waters can be accessed and explored easily. Along the edge of the lake, marsh, and grassland, vegetation provides staging and breeding habitat for fascinating wildlife species. Northern harriers, sandhill cranes, great blue herons, egrets, American white pelicans, Canada geese, and many species of waterfowl nest here during summer. During winter, coyotes hunt for small rodents living under the snow. Cutthroat, rainbow, and lake trout inhabit Bear Lake.

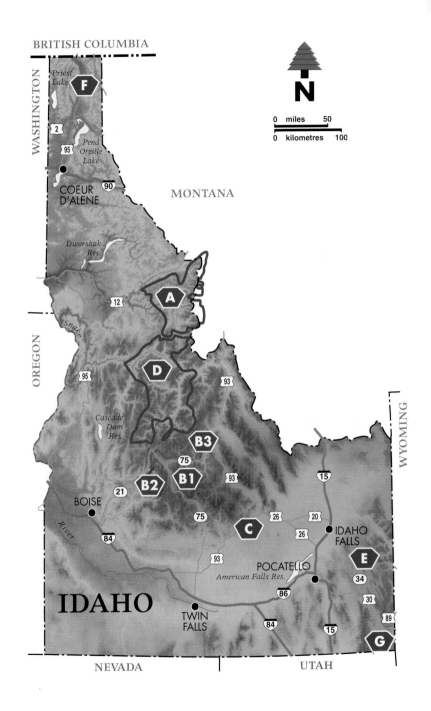

Wyoming

A YELLOWSTONE NATIONAL PARK (3472 MI²/8990 KM²)

The largest park in the lower 48 states brings volcanic natural forces alive with 10,000 exploding, bubbling, and steaming geothermal geysers, hot springs, steam vents, and mud-pots. Yellowstone is also blessed with an incredible diversity of colorful flowers, trees, and shrubs, and dynamic communities of wild animals.

B GRAND TETON NATIONAL PARK (480 MI²/1243 KM²)

Composed of rock estimated to have been formed 2.5–3.5 billion years ago during the Precambrian Era, the Grand Tetons and Jackson Hole rank among the oldest formations in the Rocky Mountain Cordillera. The 42 mi (67 km) Teton Park Scenic Loop Drive is by far the most popular way of accessing the area's scenic viewpoints and wildlife viewing hotspots. Signal Mountain Summit, Oxbow Bend, Snake River, Jenny Lake, Willow Flats, and Cascade Canyon all provide fascinating wildlife opportunities.

C NATIONAL ELK REFUGE (40 MI²/100 KM²)

From November through to May, approximately 7500 elk, or 'wapiti,' converge onto this valley of grasslands and forest to spend the winter. During various months of the year, the refuge supports a wide range of plant and animal species, including long-tailed weasel, badger, Uinta ground squirrel, Barrow's goldeneye, cinnamon teal, trumpeter swan, bald eagle, long-billed curlew, asters, larkspurs, and daisies.

D FOSSIL BUTTE NATIONAL MONUMENT (>12 MI²/>33 KM²)

This monument protects the remnants of Wyoming's ancient past. Crocodiles, giant turtles, palm and cypress trees, and now long-extinct fish once lived in a large lake estimated to have existed here about 50 million years ago. Now this area's dry, high desert habitats support coyotes, white-tailed jackrabbits, and sagebrush, while wetter areas provide for moose, golden-mantled ground squirrels, Wilson's warblers, and cottonwoods. Taking fossils from the park and camping overnight are not permitted.

E1 TETON **E2** GROS VENTRE WILDERNESSES (>1000 MI²/>2600 KM²)

Connecting the high mountains of the Continental Divide in Bridger–Teton National Forest to those in Grand Teton National Park, these wildernesses provide prime habitat for grizzly bear, bighorn sheep, mountain lion, fisher, American dipper, belted kingfisher, northern goshawk, northern flicker, American redstart, cutthroat trout, anise swallowtail, scarlet paintbrush, common harebell, and pink wintergreen. Recreationalists should use minimal impact techniques to reduce unnecessary disturbances.

F CLOUD PEAK WILDERNESS (295 MI²/764 KM²)

Established along the crest of the Bighorn Mountains, this wild place offers 150 miles of maintained trails. Pikas, bighorn sheep, yellow-bellied marmots, sharp-shinned hawks, yellow-rumped warblers, rainbow trout, daisies, asters, and saxifrages are only a few of the many species to observe and appreciate here.

G SEEDSKADEE NATIONAL WILDLIFE REFUGE & THE FONTENELLE 'MIGRANT TRAP' (>22 MI²/>58 KM²)

For early settlers, this flattened region represented the easiest route for crossing the Rockies. Established in exchange for flooding the Green River to create the Flaming Gorge Reservoir, Seedskadee is a haven for beavers, raptors, herons, waterfowl, ground squirrels, deer, and other species relying on grassland, sagebrush and riparian habitat. Just below the Fontenelle Dam, the river valley forms a major migratory route funneling many of the birds passing through western Wyoming past the eyes of eager onlookers.

H ENCAMPMENT WILDERNESSES

Huston Park Wilderness, Savage Run Wilderness, Platte River Wilderness, and the Encampment River Wilderness Area are all small protected areas established by the U.S. Forest Service within the Medicine Bow National Forest along the Colorado border. The Continental Divide National Scenic Trail passes through this area.

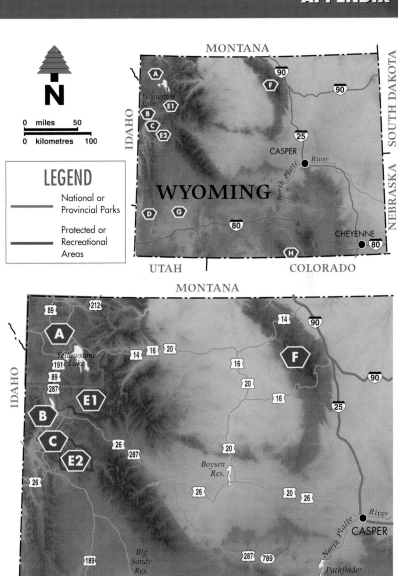

LEGEND

National or Provincial Parks

Protected or Recreational Areas

Colorado & Utah

A ROCKY MOUNTAIN NATIONAL PARK (417 MI^2/1080 KM^2)

With more than 300 mi (480 km) of trails, hikers can take in many of the park's rocky peaks, clear streams, 147 lakes, and plentiful flora and fauna. Interpretive programs are offered from June to October. Even though the tundra zone offers less than 40 frost-free growing days, upwards of 150 plant species may be found competing for survival in the high alpine.

B BLACK CANYON OF THE GUNNISON NATIONAL MONUMENT (20 MI^2/53 KM^2)

Up to 2000 ft (610 m) tall canyon cliffs tower over the wild, carving Gunnison River and create awesome and exhilarating vistas. Ruby-crowned kinglets, ravens, mountain chickadees, western tanagers, and western scrub-jays are common sights along Warner Point Trail. Douglas-fir, saskatoon, piñon pine, juniper, American dipper, striped skunk, mountain cottontail, and pine-gopher snake are also here.

C MESA VERDE NATIONAL PARK (79 MI^2/204 KM^2)

The spectacular, ancient Anasazi cliff-dwellings of Mesa Verde stand like sentinels guarding an invisible southern gateway to the Rockies. Mystery shrouds the abandoned settlement set among dramatic flat-topped mesas below the San Juan Mountains. During guided hikes to the ruins, watch for broad-tailed hummingbirds, mule deer, gray foxes, western terrestrial garter snakes, and short-horned lizards.

D GREAT SAND DUNES NATIONAL MONUMENT (56 MI^2/145 KM^2)

Visit the Great Sand Dunes at night to meet kangaroo rats, mountain cottontails, coyotes, bobcats, striped skunks, and burrowing owls engaged in their survival tactics. Mid-day views are dominated by stubborn plants growing on dune edges and by sightings of northern flickers, rock squirrels, and broad-tailed hummingbirds. As each day draws to a close, the sun sets the dunes on fire.

E1 BIG BLUE WILDERNESS AREA (156 MI^2/403 KM^2) **E2** POWDERHORN WILDERNESS AREA (94 MI^2/243 KM^2)

Tall, stunning peaks, beautiful lakes, fragrant wildflowers, and abundant wildlife characterize these wilderness areas. Trailheads are generally via U.S. Forest Service Trails. Lower-elevation trails are often used by 4x4 vehicles, while higher elevations are generally less disturbed and are alive with the sounds of wildlife.

F GOLDEN GATE CANYON STATE PARK (>4 MI^2/12 KM^2)

This foothills park just west of Denver is an excellent spot for meeting summer songbirds, such as lazuli bunting, mountain chickadee, mountain bluebird, tree swallow, western tanager, and dark-eyed junco. The visitor center has a trout viewing pond, and Ralston Creek has a beaver viewing deck. Numerous trails lead to flower-filled meadows and through mixed woodlands of conifer and deciduous aspen.

G ARAPAHO NATIONAL WILDLIFE REFUGE & ILLINOIS RIVER MOOSE VIEWING SITE (>28 MI^2/>73 KM^2)

The irrigated meadows, open ponds, and river within this sanctuary are excellent habitat for moose, muskrats, beavers, northern harriers, soras, colorful butterflies, dragonflies, waterfowl, and shorebirds. Adjacent sagebrush flats and grassy knolls provide habitat for pronghorn, Wyoming ground squirrels, black-tailed jackrabbits, kestrels, songbirds, and various plants.

H DINOSAUR NATIONAL MONUMENT, COLORADO & UTAH (298 MI^2/772 KM^2)

Flowing through deep canyons at the base of the Uinta Mountains, the Yampa River joins the Green River, whose vast waters slowly erode the ancient river valley to expose over 1600 dinosaur bones from the Jurassic Period. Dinosaur is one of few places in the Rockies where prehistoric clues (dinosaur bones) and aboriginal clues (pictographs and petroglyphs) blend together with modern natural communities.

I TIMPANOGOS CAVE NATIONAL MONUMENT, UTAH (250 ACRES/101 HA)

This monument was established to preserve the colorful limestone cavern on the side of Mount Timpanogos. Open to visitors from Memorial Day to Labor Day, a three-hour hike and tour of the cave gives you a memorable view of the cave's spectacular helietites (formations that are created by water) growing in all directions throughout the cave.

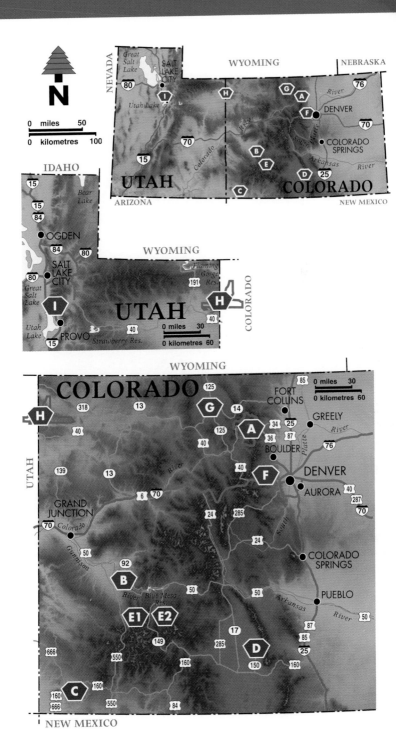

New Mexico

A BANDELIER NATIONAL MONUMENT (51 MI²/132 KM²)

Lower desert-like communities are full of sagebrush and cactus, leading up to piñon-juniper woodlands that finally yield to high-elevation forests dominated by Engelmann spruce and white fir. These communities, along with grasslands, shrublands, and riparian canyons, provide excellent habitat for butterflies, broad-tailed hummingbirds, Say's phoebes, chipping sparrows, Wilson's warblers, ringtails, and rock squirrels.

B CAPULIN VOLCANO NATIONAL MONUMENT (1 MI²/3 KM²)

The crater rim of this extinct volcano towers more than 1500 ft (457 m) over the surrounding Great Plains. A sturdy pair of boots, lots of water, and 1–3 free hours are recommended for exploring the symmetrical cinder cone's scenery and natural communities. Three distinct habitat zones—grasslands, scrub oak woodlands, and piñon-juniper woodlands—support a variety of birds, reptiles, and mammals, including spotted towhees, rock wrens, eastern short-horned lizards, and mule deer.

achene: a seed-like fruit, e.g., sunflower seed
altricial: animals who are helpless at birth or hatching
annual: plants live for only one year or growing season
aquatic: water frequenting
arboreal: tree frequenting

basal leaf: a leaf arising at the base of a plant
benthic: bottom feeding
bract: a leaf-like structure arising at the base of a flower or inflorescence
bracteole: a small bract borne on a leaf stalk
brood parasite: a bird that parasitizes other bird's nests by laying its eggs and abandoning them for the parasitized birds to raise, e.g., brown-headed cowbird

calyx: the collective of sepals
cambium: inner layers of tissue that transport nutrients up and down the plant stalk or trunk
capsules: a dry splitting fruit
carnivorous: feeding primarily on meat
carrion: decomposing animal matter or carcass
catkin: a spike of small flowers
compound leaf: a leaf separated into 2 or more divisions called leaflets
coniferous: cone-bearing. Seed (female) and pollen (male) cones are borne on the same tree in different locations.
crepuscular: active primarily at dusk and dawn
cryptic coloration: a type of camouflage designed to conceal by resembling the background

deciduous: a tree whose leaves turn color and shed annually
defoliating: dropping of the leaves
diurnal: active primarily during the day
dorsal: the top or back
drupe: a fleshy fruit with a stony pit, e.g., peach, cherry

echolocation: navigation by rebounding sound waves off of objects to target or avoid them
ecological niche: an ecological role filled by a species
ecoregion: distinction between regions based upon geology, climate, biodiversity, elevation, and soil composition
ectoparasites: skin parasites
ectotherm: an animal that regulates its body temperature behaviorally from external sources of heat, i.e., from the sun
endotherm: an animal which regulates its body temperature internally
estivate: a state of inactivity and a slowing of the metabolism to permit survival in extended periods of high temperatures and inadequate water supply
evergreen: having green leaves through winter; not deciduous

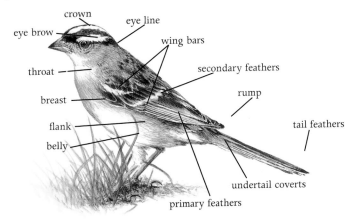

crown
eye line
eye brow
wing bars
throat
secondary feathers
breast
rump
flank
tail feathers
belly
undertail coverts
primary feathers

exoskeleton: a hard outer encasement to provide protection and points of attachment for muscles

food web: the elaborated, interconnected feeding relationships of living organisms in an ecosystem

habitat: the physical area in which an organism lives

hawking: feeding behavior where a bird leaves a perch, snatches its prey in mid-air, and returns to its previous perch

herbaceous: feeding primarily on vegetation

hibernate: a state of decreased metabolism and body temperature and slowed heart and respiratory rates to permit survival during long periods or cold temperature and diminished food supply

hinds: female elk

hips: a berry-like structure

hybrids: the offspring from a cross between parents belonging to different varieties or subspecies, sometimes between different subspecies or genera

incubate: keeping eggs at relatively constant temperature until they hatch

insectivore: feeding primarily on insects

invertebrate: animals lacking backbones, e.g., worms, slugs, crayfish, shrimps

involucral bract: one of several bracts that form a whorl subtending a flower or flower cluster

keys: winged fruits

larva: immature forms of an animal that differ from the adult

leaflet: a division of a compound leaf

lobate: having each toe individually webbed

lobe: a projecting part of a leaf or flower, usually rounded

(figure labels: node, ventral side, veins, dorsal side, blade, leaf stalk, teeth, stipule, vein (net-veined), cleft, vein (parallel-veined), lobe)

metabolic rate: the rate of chemical processes in an organism

metamorphosis: the developmental transformation of an animal from larval to sexually mature adult stage

myccorhizal fungi: a fungi that has a mutually beneficial relationship with the roots of some seed plants

neo-tropical migrant: a bird that nests in North America, but overwinters in the New World tropics

nocturnal: active primarily at night

node: a slightly enlarged section of a stem where leaves or branches originate

nutlet: a small, hard, 1-seeded fruit that remains closed

omniverous: feeding on both plants and animals

ovoid: egg-shaped

pappus: the modified calyx of the composites, consisting of awns, scales, or bristles at the apex of the achene

parasite: a relationship between two species where one benefits at the expense of the other

patagium: skin forming a flight membrane

pelage: fur or hair of mammals

perennial: a plant that lives for several years

photosynthesis: conversion of CO_2 and water into sugars via energy of the sun

pollen: the tiny grains produced in the anthers which contain the male reproductive cells

pollen cone: male cone that produces pollen

pome: a fruit with a core, e.g., apple

precocial: animals who are active at birth or hatching

proboscis: elongated tubular and flexible mouthpart of many insects

redds: spawing nests

resinous: bearing resin, usually causing stickiness

rhizome: a horizontal underground stem

riparian: riverbank

rookery: a colony of nests

runner: a slender stolon or prostrate stem rooting at the nodes or the tip

seed cone: female cone that produces seeds

sepal: the outer, usually green, leaf-like structures that protect the flower bud and are located at the base of an open flower

spur: a pointed projection

stamen: the pollen-bearing organ of a flower

stigma: a receptive tip in a flower that receives pollen

stolon: a long branch or stem that runs along the ground and often propogates more plants

subnivean: below the surface of the snow

suckering: a method of tree and shrub reproduction when shoots arise from an underground stem

taproot: a main large root of a plant from which smaller roots arise, e.g., carrot

terrestrial: land frequenting

toothed leaf: a leaf with small lobes

torpor: a state of physical inactivity

tragus: a prominant structure of the outer ear of bats

tundra: a high altitude ecological zone at the northernmost limits of plant growth, where plants are reduced to shrubby or matlike growth

ungulate: an animal that has hooves

ventrally: of or on the abdomen (belly)

vermiculations: wavy patterned makings

vertebrate: an animal possessing a backbone

vibrisae: bristle-like feathers growing about the beak of birds to aid in catching insects

whorl: a circle of leaves or flowers about a stem

wooly: bearing long or matted hairs

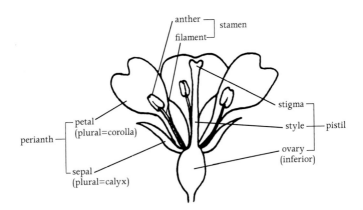

REFERENCES

Acorn, J.H. 1993. *Butterflies of Alberta*. Lone Pine Publishing, Edmonton.

Andrews, R., and R. Righter. 1992. *Colorado Birds: A Reference to their Distribution and Habitat*. Denver Museum of Natural History, Denver.

Baxter, G.T., and M.D. Stone. 1980. *Amphibians and Reptiles of Wyoming*. Wyoming Game and Fish Department, Cheyenne.

Behler, J.L., and F.W. King. 1994. *Field Guide to North American Reptiles and Amphibians* (Revised Edition). National Audubon Society. Alfred A. Knopf, New York.

Behnke, R.J. 1992. *Native Trout of Western North America*. American Fisheries Society Monograph 6. American Fisheries Society, Bethesda, Maryland.

Bird, C.D., G.J. Hilchie, N.G. Kondla, E.M. Pike and F.A.H. Sperling. 1995. *Alberta Butterflies*. The Provincial Museum of Alberta, Edmonton.

Boschung, H.T., Jr., J.D. Williams, D.W. Gotshall, D.K. Caldwell, M.C. Caldwell, C. Nehring and J. Verner. 1997. *Field Guide to North American Fishes, Whales, and Dolphins*. National Audubon Society. Alfred A. Knopf, New York.

Brayshaw, T.C. 1996. *Trees and Shrubs of British Columbia*. UBC Press, Vancouver.

Brown, C.J.D. 1971. *Fishes of Montana*. Big Sky Books, Montana State University, Bozeman.

Burt, W.H., and R.P. Grossenheider. 1987. *A Field Guide to the Mammals*. Peterson Field Guides. Houghton Mifflin Company, Boston.

Carter, 1988. *Trees and Shrubs of Colorado*. Johnson Books, Boulder, Colorado.

Craighead, John J., Frank C. Craighead, Jr., and Ray J. Davis. 1963. *A Field Guide To Rocky Mountain Wildflowers*. The Peterson Field Guide Series. Houghton Mifflin Company, Boston.

Ehrlich, P.R., D.S. Dobkin and D. Wheye. 1988. *The Birder's Handbook: A Field Guide to the Natural History of North American Birds*. Simon & Shuster Inc., Toronto.

Farrand, J., ed. 1983. *The Audubon Society Master Guide to Birding*. Vols. 1–3. Alfred A. Knopf, New York.

Flora of North America Editorial Committee (eds.). 1993. *Flora of North America North of Mexico*. Vol. 2. Pteridophytes and Gymnosperms. Oxford University Press, New York.

Forsyth, A. 1985. *Mammals of the Canadian Wild*. Camden House Publishing Ltd, East Camden, Ontario.

Gadd, Ben. 1995. *Handbook of the Canadian Rockies* (Second Edition). Corax Press, Jasper, Alberta.

Gregory, P.T., and R.W. Campbell. 1987. *The Reptiles of British Columbia*. Royal British Columbia Museum Handbook. Royal British Columbia Museum, Victoria.

Harrington, H.D. 1964. *Manual of the Plants of Colorado*. Sage Books, Swallow Press Incorporated, Chicago.

Kaufman, K. 1996. *Lives of North American Birds*. Peterson Natural History Companions. Houghton Mifflin Company, Boston.

Kuijt, J. 1982. *A Flora of Waterton Lakes National Park*. The University of Alberta Press, Edmonton.

MacKinnon, A., J. Pojar and R. Coupe. 1992. *Plants of Northern British Columbia*. Lone Pine Publishing, Edmonton.

Moss, E.H. 1983. *Flora of Alberta* (Second Edition, revised by J.G. Packer). University of Toronto Press, Toronto.

Nagorsen, D.W. 1996. *Opossums, Shrews and Moles of British Columbia*. Royal British Columbia Museum Handbook. UBC Press, Vancouver.

Nagorsen, D.W., and R.M. Brigham. 1993. *Bats of British Columbia*. Royal British Columbia Museum Handbook. UBC Press, Vancouver.

Nelson, R.A. 1992. *Handbook of Rocky Mountain Plants* (Fourth Edition, revised by R.L. Williams). Roberts Rinehart Publishers, Niwot, Colorado.

Newfield, N.L., and B. Nielsen. 1996. *Hummingbird Gardens: Attracting Nature's Jewels to Your Backyard*. Chapters Publishing Ltd., Shelburne, Vermont.

Paetz, M., and J. Nelson. 1992. *The Fishes of Alberta*. The University of Alberta Press, Edmonton.

Parish, R., R. Coupe and D. Lloyd (eds.). 1996. *Plants of Southern Interior British Columbia*. Lone Pine Publishing, Edmonton.

Pattie, D.L., and R.S. Hoffmann. 1992. *Mammals of the North American Parks and Prairies* (Second Edition). Self-published, Edmonton.

Pesman, M.W. 1988. *Meet the Natives - A Beginner's Guide too Rocky Mountain Wildflowers, Trees and Shrubs* (Eighth Edition). Pruett Publishing, Boulder, Colorado.

Porsild, A.E. 1979. *Rocky Mountain Wild Flowers*. National Museum of Natural Science. National Museums of Canada, Ottawa.

Reader's Digest. 1990. *Book of North American Birds*. The Reader's Digest Association, Inc., Montreal.

Russell, A.P., and A.M. Bauer. 1993. *The Amphibians and Reptiles of Alberta*. The University of Alberta Press, Edmonton.

Rydberg, P.A. 1917. *Flora of the Rocky Mountains and Adjacent Plains*. New York Botanical Garden., New York.

Ryser, F.A., Jr. 1985. *Birds of the Great Basin: A Natural History*. University of Nevada Press, Reno.

Scott, S.S., ed. 1987. *Field Guide to the Birds of North America* (Second Edition). National Geographic Society, Washington D.C.

Scotter, G.W., and T.J. Ulrich. 1995. *Mammals of the Canadian Rockies*. Fifth House Publishers Ltd., Saskatoon.

Sheldon, I. 1997. *Animal Tracks of the Rockies*. Lone Pine Publishing, Edmonton.

Simpson, J.C., and R.L. Wallace. 1982. *Fishes of Idaho*. The University Press of Idaho, Moscow.

Smith, H. 1993. *Alberta Mammals: An Atlas and Guide*. The Provincial Museum of Alberta, Edmonton.

Stebbins, R.C. 1985. *A Field Guide to Western Reptiles and Amphibians*. The Peterson Field Guide Series. Houghton Mifflin Company, Boston.

Stokes, D.W., and L.Q. Stokes. 1996. *Stokes Field Guide to Birds: Western Region* (First Edition). Little, Brown & Company (Canada) Limited, Toronto.

Sublette, J.E., M.D. Hatch and M. Sublette. 1990. *The Fishes of New Mexico*. University of New Mexico Press, Albuquerque.

Ulrich, T.J. 1990. *Mammals of the Northern Rockies*. Mountain Press Publishing Company, Missoula.

Wassink, J.L. 1993. *Mammals of the Central Rockies*. Mountain Press Publishing Company, Missoula.

Weber, W.A. 1972. *Rocky Mountain Flora*. Colorado Associated University Press, Boulder, Colorado.

Whitaker, J.O., Jr. 1996. *Field Guide to North American Mammals* (Revised Edition.). National Audubon Society. Alfred A. Knopf, New York.

Wilkinson, K. 1990. *Trees and Shrubs of Alberta*. Lone Pine Publishing, Edmonton.

Page numbers in **bold** indicate primary species.

LONE PINE

Lone Pine has the Rockies covered!
Look for these terrific titles at a bookstore or a Lone Pine book rack near you.

PLANTS OF THE ROCKY MOUNTAINS
By Linda Kershaw, Andy MacKinnon & Jim Pojar

Over 1300 species of trees, shrubs, wildflowers, grasses, ferns, mosses and lichens are described and illustrated with more than 900 color photographs and 700 line drawings.

1-55105-088-9 • $5^{1}/_{2}$" x $8^{1}/_{2}$" • 384 pages • Softcover • $26.95 CDN • $19.95 US

BIRDS OF THE ROCKY MOUNTAINS
By Chris Fisher

This lavishly illustrated guide contains more than 320 common and interesting birds of the Rockies. Each is brought to life by colorful illustrations and descriptive text. Includes Alberta, British Columbia, Montana, Idaho, Wyoming, Utah, Colorado and New Mexico.

1-55105-091-9 • $5^{1}/_{2}$"x $8^{1}/_{2}$" • 336 pages • Softcover • $24.95 CDN • $19.95 US

ANIMAL TRACKS OF THE ROCKIES
By Ian Sheldon

Learn the track shape, stride pattern, travel habits and other fascinating facts about the animals in the Rocky Mountains. Identify any track from shrew to grizzly bear in snow, sand or mud. Contains illustrations of tracks, stride patterns and the animals themselves.

1-55105-089-7 • $4^{1}/_{4}$" x $3^{3}/_{4}$" • 160 pages • Softcover • $7.95 CDN • $5.95 US

CANADIAN ROCKIES ACCESS GUIDE (1998 REVISED EDITION)
By John Dodd & Gail Helgason

This essential guide for exploring the Rockies includes dayhikes, backpacking, boating, camping, cycling, fishing and rainy-day activities. Covers Banff, Jasper, Kootenay, Yoho, Waterton Lakes and Kananaskis parks. It's packed with maps and full-color photographs.

1-55105-176-1 • $5^{1}/_{2}$" x $8^{1}/_{2}$" • 400 pages • Softcover • $19.95 CDN • $16.95 US

Canadian Orders
1-800-661-9017 Phone
1-800-424-7173 Fax

US Orders
1-800-518-3541 Phone
1-800-548-1169 Fax

Visit our website at www.lonepinepublishing.com